D1604465

North to Danger

NORTH

TO DANGER

By VIRGIL BURFORD
as told to
WALT MOREY

THE JOHN DAY COMPANY

NEW YORK

Contents

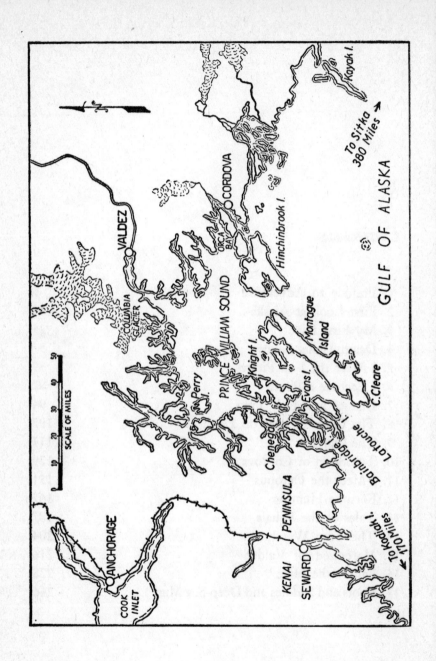

North to Danger

1

Prelude to Adventure

The day I ran away from home at the age of fourteen I did not dream I was taking the first step that would lead to a life of adventure. I only knew that my father had left and home, as I had known it, was no more. No stepfather was going to order me about, I thought bitterly. On that first trip I beat my way on foot and on freight trains into New Mexico, Arizona and California. I went hungry more than once, slept cold under bridges, and ate many a mulligan stew from a can in a hobo jungle. To this day I am amazed that I experienced no serious troubles during that time.

I was big and husky for fourteen and I could handle a team of horses. In those days no farmer asked your age or where you were from. He only asked if you could do the job.

Usually I could, and I came cheaper than a man.

When I returned home two years later, the love of adventure had taken deep root within me. I look back now and see that the things I did during those early years laid the foundation for my life in Alaska. That mental and physical training made it possible for me to face an octopus, a killer whale, the charge of a giant Kodiak bear. It saved my life on numerous occasions when I became trapped in a diving suit beneath the sea.

I soon left home again to prospect for gold with a pair of miners I had met in Idaho's Salmon River Country. That was the hardest kind of work, but I did my share. My only rewards for almost three years of climbing over mountains and swinging a pick and shovel were well-developed muscles and a knowledge of prospecting.

There were several large cattle ranches in the Salmon River Country and I decided the life of a cowboy was more to my liking. That was the big turning point in my life. I had been on a ranch almost a year when we all came to town one Saturday night. A carnival had pitched its tents at one end of Main Street and we all gravitated that way for the fun. A barker was trying to lure someone in the crowd to take on the carnival's fighter. He was a beat-up old pug who pranced about the ring throwing punches at the air.

Of course, I was in the front row. I was almost six feet then and weighed a hundred and eighty. For some reason the barker directed his spiel at me, and the boys began to push and urge me forward. The next I knew I was in the tent climbing into a pair of borrowed trunks.

I managed to stay the three rounds simply because I was stronger than my aged opponent. Afterward he confided, "Kid, you did fine. You're strong and quick, and can take a punch. Give me a month and I can teach you enough so you can take on any of these hillbillies. What do you say to coming with us?"

"Travel with the carnival as a fighter?" I asked.

"Sure—here's the situation. Right now I'm doing double

duty. A half hour from now I wrestle anybody in the crowd. Wrestling and boxing the same night is too much for a guy my age. You take the fighting and I'll teach you the tricks. I'll stick to the wrestling."

Here was a chance to travel again, to see new towns, new country and new faces, to experience new adventures. Suddenly, being a cowboy seemed the drabbest sort of life.

During the next three years with the carnival I saw a lot of country and fought almost every night. The fighting was the best training for what lay ahead. During that time I met Wilma. When we were finally married I dropped the carnival circuit.

Together we opened a small restaurant, but times were hard. That venture lasted just a year. I held a number of short-time jobs after that, in the harvest fields, on farms and in logging camps. They barely paid our expenses.

Then, one night, a carnival came to town. Of course we went. They had a fighter and again the barker was trying to pull a crowd. Once again I was in the front row. It was a carbon copy of that first time, except that now I was older and knew more. The barker's voice brought back pleasant memories of my own carnival life. The next thing I knew I was again climbing into borrowed trunks.

The fighter came in and asked, "Do you want to work, fellow, or do a little business?" How often I had asked that question of some hopeful. It meant, "Do we fight on the level or give them a show?"

"I would like to do business," I said. "I think we could pack them in on a re-match. . . . But my wife is out front so I guess we work."

"So you know the score?"

I told him the outfit I had worked with. For ten minutes we had a fine shoptalk while they sold tickets outside. Finally he said, "This was a good racket while it lasted, but now it's dying out. I'm quitting next week."

"What will you do then?" I asked.

"I'm going North, to Alaska. There's a lot of work and fishing going on around a town called Cordova—naval installations, air strips, things like that. I got a letter from a friend up there and he's making up to eighty and a hundred dollars a week as a carpenter."

"You're sure of this?" I asked, beginning to get excited.

"Of course. His letter is around here someplace. Jim says jobs are so plentiful they practically reach out and grab you as you walk down the street. So that's where I'm going next week."

A minute later we were called into the ring.

He gave me as rough a time as I have ever had, but I stuck it out and collected my money. As I was about to leave, he said, "You're not rich, or you wouldn't get punched around like this for a few bucks. Why don't you give that Alaska deal some thought? It's a fine chance to make a stake."

Wilma and I talked it over for several days. Finally we decided that if I could get a job in Alaska I could send home more money than I could ever make in Idaho. "At least we will be saving a little," Wilma said. "We certainly need a stake."

Wilma is an understanding wife. I am sure she consented to my going North because she knew the fever was on me and I had to explore beyond the next hill. If I could do this, and save some money too, it would be all to the good.

Four days after the carnival, and carrying every cent we

could scrape up, I was on a plane for Alaska. I had high hopes it would prove to be the "land of opportunity." I did not dream that I was rushing headlong into unbelievable adventures in which more than once my life would hang in the balance.

2

First Look at Alaska

My introduction to Alaska was cold and drizzly. I arrived in Anchorage at five A.M. At ten I stood on the edge of a dingy little airfield on the outskirts of town where a bush pilot was to fly me to Cordova. It was a gray day. Fog banners drifted across the field. The Cook Inlet tide flats were a musty stench on the damp morning.

I had a ticket for Cordova in one hand, a suitcase in the other. There was one dollar left in my pocket. From here, I figured, any direction my fortunes took had to be up.

We took off—two other men and a woman with a baby and a dog in a box, besides the pilot and me—in an overloaded wreck of a plane. Twenty minues later we sighted the first blue bays of Prince William Sound, with a white boat about an inch long. Close on our left a ragged line of snow-covered mountains marched along a leaden horizon. Glaciers wound between brush and tundra mountains like white rivers frozen in the act of plunging into the sea. The pilot tipped the plane's nose down toward a flat meadow. "Let's go bear hunting," he shouted. "Kind of early but maybe we can find one out."

We whipped low across the meadow, jumped over a mountain, roared down the opposite slope into a deep valley, raced the length of the valley, banked around a huge shoulder of earth and fled across a flat tundra plain. There were no bears out today. I was destined to tramp these hills and valleys later, and to find more Kodiak bears than I bargained for.

Two hours later we passed low over a postage-stamp town plastered against the base of a snow-covered mountain. A dock thrust into the bay with half a hundred boats moored along its length. It was Cordova.

We landed on the beach of a lake, a mile behind the town, and all of us crowded into an old Chevrolet cab that took us to town and let us out before one of the bars. The driver said, "That'll be a buck." I thought he meant a dollar each, so I gave him my last one. The woman disappeared down the street, the baby in one arm, the dog box under the other. The two men went into the bar and climbed on stools. I stood on the street and looked around.

Cordova was an old town. Some fifty or sixty weather-stained wooden buildings made up the two blocks of Main Street. The sidewalks were wooden and canted at irregular, rotting angles. The street was gray mud and gravel. Homes clung without seeming pattern to the rocky and brushy mountain above the town. The bay lay a hundred or so feet below the street.

I looked about for the promised construction activity. There was none. In fact, Cordova might have passed for a ghost town. I was the only person on the dripping wind-swept street.

I turned into the bar. It was old, too. The floor was wooden, foot-chewed. A long bar ran the length of the room; the

back bar was stacked with an imposing array of bottles and
a huge mirror.

When the bartender came I said, "I heard there was a lot
of work going on here."

"Work?" he asked.

"Construction, fishing," I said.

"You're three months early for fishing. The construction
is all at Sitka and south."

"None here at all?"

"You saw the town. You see any?"

So the jobs will reach out and grab you as you walk down
the street! I thought.

"How far is it to Sitka?" I asked.

"You flew over it coming up. Go back to Anchorage and
take a plane south from there. Six, seven hundred miles."

"Flying is out."

"Why? Busted?"

"Flat."

"That's too bad." He swished a towel across the bar.

A man entered, straddled a stool and called for a drink.
He had a month's growth of black beard, wore a gray turtle-
neck sweater and hip boots rolled beneath the knees. I guessed
he was somewhere in the thirties.

The bartender came back from mixing his drink and said,
"That's George Shore. He's taking his *Lady Claire* to Ketchi-
kan. Maybe you can make a deal with him to take you to
Sitka."

George Shore looked at me with bright black eyes and
said, "We could use a cook."

"I can cook well enough for myself, if that will do," I said.

He sized me up. "You look healthy. It's a deal. There'll be

four of us counting yourself. Three meals a day. Nothing fancy. Coffee on the stove all the time—that's a must. You're lucky! I'd have been gone in another ten minutes." He grinned. "We've got time for just one more drink. What'll you have?"

So here I was, at my destination less than half an hour, broke, not yet hungry, heading back over the trail I had just traveled, and in charge of a galley filled with grub. That crazy morning from Anchorage to Cordova set a pattern of events that followed me all through my Alaskan days.

Four days and twelve meals later we pulled into the dock at Sitka. I stepped ashore and went up the street with my suitcase. I was still broke. But things looked different in Sitka. The street was packed with construction workers and I had seen marine installations and docks abuilding as we entered the harbor.

Sitka is situated on Baranof Island, facing on the open sea. Its harbor is protectively ringed by snow-capped, forest-draped mountains. Mt. Edgecumbe, an extinct volcano, almost a mile high, makes an unmistakable landmark in Sitka Bay. This is the oldest historical town in Alaska. The business district is about three blocks long and, like Cordova, composed of old wooden buildings, wooden sidewalks and mud and gravel streets. For more than half a century, under the name New Archangel, Sitka was the chief port and seat of government for Russian America. The marks of Russia are still visible. There is the Russo-Greek church built in 1816 with its high spired dome and Russian Bible bound in solid gold leaf. About six miles from town is Old Sitka, or Fort Archangel Gabriel, founded in 1799. The fort was captured by the natives in a battle in 1802, recaptured by the Russians two years later, after which they moved the town to its present site. A Russian school and a great log warehouse are still standing. The town is overrun with Russian names and with broad, flat Russian features and pale skins. But the native Alaskan shows through in jet-black hair and snapping black eyes.

My carnival fighter friend back in Idaho must have been thinking of Sitka. In the middle of the second block I found a construction office. Fifteen minutes later I was a pile buck and was aboard the company's work boat headed for an island fourteen miles out from town.

I had been there about a week when one day the pile driver broke the cable that raises the hammer and that ton-sized steel fist crashed from the peak of the rig into the sea. Next day a diver arrived in a small boat to try to recover it.

I got the job of handling the underwater telephone. Another pile buck, that I knew only as Joe, who always referred to the Pacific as the "Old Lady," handled the air line. "I used to do some diving," he said. "Kind of like to get my hand in again." He was about fifty-five, long and lean as a piling and about as clean. Joe always had half a plug of tobacco in one cheek and half a can of snuff in the other. "To keep me balanced when I walk a stringer," he explained.

The diver was a good-natured, grinning fellow. He showed us how to start the compressor, the poundage he wanted, how to help him on with the suit. Joe kept saying, "Sure, sure. I know. Little different from the kind I used, but I get you." I screwed the face plate shut when he was ready, said into the telephone, "Okay," and watched fascinated as he shuffled ponderously to the rail and stepped off into the sea.

The same fascination held me that has held men for centuries, the thrill of adventure, danger, the lure of an unknown world. For a minute I watched his bubbles streaming back to the surface; then I asked, "Say, what is it like down there?"

A chuckle came over the phone, "Somebody forgot to pull the plug. There's water all over the floor."

Joe said in a disgusted voice, "Relax, Virg, he's just another diver."

I asked, "Why did you quit diving?"

"Just got fed up. Besides, the 'Old Lady' was after me every time I went down. She almost got me more than once. Man's only got so much luck, I figure. I quit before I used all mine up."

"How much do you think this diver makes a day?"

"Hundred bucks a day—or a dive. Maybe more."

"A hundred!" I had worked a whole month for less back home in Idaho. Here this diver was doing a job I was sure I could learn, and wallowing in a golden rut. I decided right then, he and I were going to have a heart-to-heart talk.

The diver popped to the surface an hour later and announced he was through for the day. He had not found the hammer. We got the suit off him and he headed for Sitka.

That night Joe had a gang clustered around him in front of the bunkhouse listening to diving experiences in open-mouthed awe. As I passed once I heard, "We're down about thirty feet, see, nailing braces on the pilings. This kid gets his air line fouled up and I go down to help him out. I stick my head around the opposite side of the piling from him and it scares him so bad, darned if he don't bite me." The rest must have been just as good. He held that crowd for two hours.

Next day the diver's eyes were red-rimmed and watery,
and his breath was strong enough to lean against. He stumbled about the deck insisting he felt fine. "I could dive
this thing with my eyes shut. Let's get going." We put the
suit on him and he staggered to the rail and fell into the sea.
I watched his bubbles boiling up in the same place for ten
minutes. Then I asked, "How are you making out?"

"Fine," he mumbled. "Best bed I've had in days." He was
lying on botton trying to sober up. At that time it was believed that the fact that under pressure the body absorbs more
oxygen than normally would sober a man up quickly.

The trick did not work but he did find the hammer and
attach a cable to it for raising.

When he came up he had a hang-over that was something
to see and a disposition to match. We got the suit off to the
accompaniment of such remarks as, "This is a lousy business.
You risk your neck and they say you're robbing them. What's
a diver got to show for his work, anyhow? Carpenter builds
a house—there she is. Steelworker builds a bridge—there she
is. What has a diver got to show? Not a thing. Absolutely
not a thing." When we got the suit off he dumped us ashore
and headed for Sitka. If I wanted to talk diving with him
I knew I would have to hunt him up on my day off.

Two days later the talk went through the mess hall that
a diver had quit and they were looking for another.

That night when I hopped the work boat into Sitka Joe
was aboard. We grinned at each other. "Going to do a little
celebrating, Virg?" he asked.

"It's been almost a week since I was in town," I said.

"Same here. I left a drink there and I want to get her before somebody else does." We were both lying and knew it.

I did not like this. Joe had a definite edge over me with his experience. All the way in I brooded at one end of the cabin while Joe sprawled comfortably at the other, working industriously at his double slug of tobacco.

When we landed Joe was in no hurry and lounged on the dock talking with the skipper. I headed for the office thinking, Joe had experience. He could afford to be confident. All I had was talk. I needed a good story for a convincer and I tried to manufacture one as I went along.

The office was locked and dark. It had been open evenings before. I would wait. But a storm of half rain, half snow drove along the street, making waiting miserable. There was a bar across the street with a window that commanded a view of the office. I splashed over and went in. The place was packed and noisy. Drinks were sailing along the bar. A juke box was moaning into the din. I found a stool near the window and ordered a drink.

I was finishing the drink when Joe ambled along. He stopped and looked through the office window, then went on up the street.

A big fellow down the bar noisily bought a round of drinks and another was shoved before me. I finished that and still the windows across the street were dark.

You can't occupy a stool in a crowded bar without drinking something. So I ordered another. I sipped it, stalling for time, but it did no good. I finished that one and ordered another and another.

I was finishing this last drink when lights bloomed across the street. I hurried over.

Frank Nelson, the superintendent who had hired me, sat on the edge of a desk swinging his leg. Nelson had a dark skin and thick chest and shoulders. He looked tough as a ten-pound maul. I told him what I had heard and what I wanted. He just looked at me, waiting, so I launched into my story. I told him I had worked with divers before, that they had shown me things—I was vague about what. I said I'd been down once—back in the States, that is. I could do the job. If I couldn't, fire me. It didn't cost anything to give me a try.

"I think you can dive, too," he said surprisingly. "But I hear there's a fellow working with you who was once a diver. Naturally, he gets first chance if he wants it."

There was no arguing with that, so I said, "I guess you mean Joe. He came in tonight. We can hunt him up if you like."

We found Joe in the second bar. He was in a corner alone, scowling into a half-empty glass.

I leaned against a stool; Joe's face was getty fuzzy and my legs were turning to rubber.

Nelson came straight to the point. "I hear you're a diver," he said to Joe. "Our diver pulled out and we need another. Do you want the job?"

"Wel-l-l-l . . ." Joe fidgeted and moved his glass about.

"You want it or not?"

Joe swallowed. He rubbed the back of his neck, "As a matter of fact my diving was a little different. . . ."

"What do you mean, different? What outfit did you dive for?"

"No special outfit. Like I say—my diving was different," Joe repeated.

"How different?" Nelson was suddenly suspicious. "Maybe you're talking about a springboard," he said sarcastically.

"Wel-l-l-l, in a way . . ."

"Wh-a-a-t!" Nelson shouted. "How about all these stories I've been hearing? According to them you've raised everything but the Japanese Current."

Joe turned suddenly righteously indignant. "What else a guy got to do setting around this Godforsaken place nights? A man's got to entertain himself somehow, ain't he?"

"Oh, hell!" Nelson threw up his hands and walked out. I followed him outside and he said, "Go get a physical; if you pass, I'll give you a tryout in the morning."

In the doctor's office everything went fine until he strapped the band around my arm and pumped it up. Then he quit and began putting instruments away. "This diving calls for a lot of stamina, doesn't it?"

"Sure does," I said.

"Get squeezed by the sea sometimes?"

"Sometimes."

He went on putting instruments away. Finally I asked, "Is everything okay, Doc?"

"Your blood pressure is too high for diving," he said.

"Too high!" That was impossible. "I've had a lot of physicals," I said. "I used to do some fighting. Nothing was ever said before."

"It's too high now," he said callously.

I got into my shirt but I was not satisfied. "Doc," I asked, "what causes high blood pressure?"

"Oh, overeating, excessive excitement, alcohol. . . ."

"I had five drinks, would that cause it?"

"Possibly."

"If I got rid of the alcohol, would I be all right?"

"If that had been the original cause, yes."

My heart was climbing back out of my shoes. "If it's normal in the morning will you okay me?"

"Naturally."

"I'll see you in the morning," I said. I hit the street and headed for the nearest restaurant for black coffee.

Several hours and a half-dozen big cups of black coffee later it dawned on me that coffee, too, is a stimulant. Maybe it would have the same effect on my blood pressure as alcohol!

I knew only one way to counteract the coffee—walk it out of my system. Between then and morning I tramped miles up and down Sitka's rain- and wind-swept board walks.

When the doctor arrived I was sitting on the steps of his office waiting, bleary-eyed, weary, my aching feet on fire.

I passed this time. I am, without doubt, the only diver on record who drank himself out of and into the same job during one night.

3

My First Dive

The tryout dive was to be at nearby Japonsky Island. The island had derived its name from a crew of Japanese fishermen that had been wrecked there in 1805. Now it was the site of an American Naval Air Base. The subterranean passage from the ammunition room to the sea was plugged. I was to go down and see why.

We picked up a pair of pile bucks to handle the telephone and air line and help me dress. Nelson was along and sat in judgment on a hatch, calmly smoked and watched.

When you think of diving, a strange thing happens to your thoughts about water. Normally I would look at a body of water and think of a drink, a swim, a bath, fishing or boating. Perhaps I would think how deep it was, but I would not be concerned with that depth.

Now I sat on a box in borrowed diving dress and thought: "I have never been down; I have never even been in a suit. I have even put on this suit from memory and I'm not sure I have everything on right. All I know is what little I saw from the deck of a boat when another man made a couple of dives. On the strength of that I am going to dive. There will be thirty feet of that wet stuff over my head and I have got to breathe down there. That rubber hose is my air line. The little engine with the tank, like a home hot water tank, is the compressor that feeds me air. It is as important to my living as my heart. I wonder what it's like down there?" The only bottom I knew anything about was a couple of creeks back home. Was it rocky? Sandy? Would I sink into a hole fifty feet deep? Would I see a shark, an octopus? What should I do if I saw one? I had not thought of these questions when I applied for the job. Even the day made the job seem worse—a squally day spitting frigid rain and a bullying wind. I glanced around. The bay was plowed into whitecaps. Froth-tipped swells marched in from the misty reaches of the sea, causing the boat to pitch steadily. Suddenly the magnitude of the sea hit me and I was plain frightened.

My helpers got the compressor going and I watched the needle climb to sixty pounds. The former diver had not used a life line, being good enough to control his ascent and descent with air pressure. I used one. It was fortunate I did. One of the pile bucks smeared vinegar on all four helmet lights so they would not fog up, then set the helmet over my head and screwed the face plate shut. I was ready to dive. I mean, I was as ready as I knew how to be.

I stood there in my forty-pound lead shoes, seventy-five pounds of helmet and breastplate, eighty-pound lead belt. My straps and buckles were as tight as two strong men could draw them. Almost two hundred pounds of lead and brass dragged at me, weight that would plummet me to the bottom and hold me there. The smell of vinegar was sickening. From the confines of the helmet I looked through the face plate and a feeling of utter helplessness rushed over me. My breathing was shallow and my heart beat painfully against my ribs. Panic came into my throat. Pride was the only thing that finally got my shuffling feet to the edge of the boat.

I hesitated, listening to the steady *tunk-tunk* of the compressor, trying to remember all the things I had seen the diver do. He had adjusted the air valve, turning air into the suit, slapped his hands against his legs to make sure the suit was ballooning properly, lifted a hand in a half salute to his air-line tender, said into the telephone, "Going over," and jumped off into the sea. He had sunk about six feet, then the air in the suit had bobbed him shoulder high where he had got turned around the way he wanted to walk on bottom. Then he had hit the chin valve with his jaw and sunk from sight.

I adjusted the air valve and felt the cool breeze on the back of my neck, slapped my legs, lifted a hand to the hose tender—then just stood there. I had not the courage to jump. The hose tender waited. The man on the telephone waited. Finally I simply wiped all thought from my mind, croaked, "Going over!" and jumped straight out into the sea.

I struck with a mighty splash, shot thirty feet to bottom, landed smack on my head and knocked myself cold. I came to with the whole Pacific Ocean sitting straddle on my chest like a ton of concrete. A half-dozen fish were playing tag around the face plate, and the tender's voice was going crazy in the helmet. "Hey, you all right? You all right? Why the hell don't you answer? Diver, you okay? Hey! Hey!"

I swallowed and said, "Of course I'm all right. Why?" I tried to sound like a busy man interrupted at his work.

"Man!" he said, "you went down awful fast."

I lay there for a little, feeling the cool stream of air eddying through the helmet, watching the fish and marveling that here I was under water and breathing! Actually breathing! I could see about ten or twelve feet. The water was a dark, dirty blue-green. I imagined I could see the outline of the bottom of the boat, but I was not sure. A little above me and to the left was the subterranean passage to the ammunition room. If I had jumped six feet to the left I would have landed on it and done myself plenty of damage.

I tried to roll over but the sea sits heavy at thirty feet. I finally managed to get onto my stomach and from there to hands and knees, only to fall flat. I kept hoisting myself on all fours and collapsing. Finally I made it and got to my feet. I first looked into the passage entrance and discovered it was plugged with concrete—a seepage, doubtless, from the construction period. After that I began to take a few short, careful steps like a baby learning to walk, eyes wide for anything I could see.

I felt like a goldfish in a bowl and expected to bump into glass sides any moment. I kept reminding myself I had the whole sea to walk in.

Walking was a real problem. The pressure of the sea is tremendous. The suit was plastered tight to my body and though air poured into the helmet I was finding breathing painful, as though a giant wrestler were trying to crush my ribs. I soon learned that to walk, it was necessary to lean forward, like a fullback hitting the line, and drive against the weight of the sea.

The bottom where I had landed was silty. Crabs scuttled from beneath my lead feet, stirring up tiny clouds of sea dust. Strands of seaweed stretched toward the surface and waved languidly to the slow pull of a current. A patch of long grass bent double as if blown down by a prairie wind. Fish came out of the blue-green distance, looked me over with curious, unafraid stares, and disappeared back through the liquid wall. A big fish, a halibut about five feet long, took off from bottom with a rush. Things are so magnified under water that he looked big enough to swallow me. I felt like a slow-motion picture, and I moved that way. I was the only human in a strange and fascinating dreamworld.

The voice of the tender said into the helmet, "Did you find that subterranean passage yet?"

I said, "Yes, I've found it and I'll be up soon."

I wanted to do a little more exploring and practice with the suit. But it seemed to be getting harder to breathe, I was getting tired and sweat was trickling down my face.

I intended to go up as the diver had, inflate the suit and bob to the surface. I turned on more air but nothing happened. I was nailed solid to bottom. This was no time or place to experiment so I called them and said to haul me up.

It is a tremendously exhilarating sensation to come up from your first dive. The air seems sweeter, the day brighter. The world is suddenly a wonderful place to be alive in even if the rain is freezing and the wind cuts you in half. You have not returned from the dead, but from the bottom of the sea, no less.

While my two helpers stripped off the suit, I told Nelson what was wrong with the passage. He nodded, "We can come out with a jackhammer and knock it loose." Not a word about whether I had a job diving or not. In view of my headlong plunge off the boat, I had not the nerve to ask.

During the run back to Sitka I got in the cabin alone with

the suit and discovered why I had not been able to inflate
and float up. The chin valve was stuck open and the air
had escaped as fast as it had been pumped into the helmet.
The air had not circulated throughout the rest of the suit.
That accounted for the painfulness of my breathing. The
protective padding of air pressure I should have had inside
the suit to counteract the sea's pressure had not been there.
I had been getting squeezed. Luckily that dive had not been
sixty feet and I had not gone down into a hole. The sea's
tremendous pressure would have crushed my body to jelly.

When we pulled into the dock Nelson came into the cabin
and said, "You might as well stay aboard. We'll be using this
boat for diving. I'll bring in your pile-bucking check. You
can buy this suit. The diver won't be needing it." He hesitated, and it seemed the faintest smile touched his lips. "There
won't be any more dives for a few days, so if you want to
practice around the bay a little, go ahead."

For just a minute, after he had gone, I wanted to yell for
the sheer joy of letting off steam. Then the seriousness of the
job came home to me. I had been lucky today. I would not
always be so lucky. Now that I had the job I must learn to
dive if I meant to stay alive. "All right," I told myself, "I
can learn." I know now that was the confidence of complete
ignorance.

The rain had stopped and the driving wind had sunk to a
breeze. At four o'clock daylight was fading out of a gray
sky. The snow-capped ridges ringing Sitka Bay came out of
the mist. Night came swiftly and the water turned a dense
black.

I was out early next morning. I wanted to get in as many
practice dives as possible before Nelson called me for a regu-

lar dive. It was no trick to pick up a couple of men to go along and handle lines. People are fascinated by the thought of a man going beneath the sea and are always anxious to help.

I headed for a secluded, shallow spot and anchored. There we got the compressor going and the boys dressed me in the suit. Diving gear consists of a heavy canvas suit with rubber cuffs and neck. The shoes are an inch thick, lead soled and weigh twenty pounds each. The breastplate and helmet weigh seventy-five, lead belt eighty. All told the suit and I weighed four hundred pounds. The helmet locks on the breastplate with a one-eighth turn and has a safety lock behind. Divers have been drowned when the safety lock was broken or forgotten and the helmet was blown off by the air pressure inside. There are earphones, and a mike is fastened in the helmet a few inches above the mouth. The helmet has four six-inch lights of quarter-inch shatterproof glass with crossbars. One light is directly ahead, one on each side and one on top of the helmet. The air is pumped in at the back of the helmet and circulates throughout the suit.

The air pressure in the suit must match, and preferably slightly exceed, the sea's pressure. This is the diver's only protection from the sea's killing squeeze. Lose the air in the suit for a second in deep water, and divers have a saying for the result. "They bury the helmet." The diver's body is squeezed into a jellylike mass and forced upward into the helmet.

The diver keeps the inside pressure counteracting the outside by bumping the chin valve to eject excess air that is constantly pouring into the suit. The valve also acts as the elevator between the surface and the bottom of the sea. To dive, the diver ejects the air that keeps him afloat; then he sinks. To rise, he lets air accumulate and floats smoothly up.

I knew little of this that day I went down for my second dive. But I dived long hours in the days that followed and I learned. I am sure Nelson knew what I was doing, but he said nothing. Everything I learned during that time was by trial and error. Now, I am strong for that sort of teaching, but in the case of diving, while there can be plenty of trial, there had better be few errors, and none of those big. Death is a diver's constant companion down below, eternally waiting, just the thickness of the face plate away.

There is a tremendous fascination about diving. Imagine—fifty, a hundred, two hundred feet down—your lead-shod feet tramping the hills and valleys of another world, a world old as time, crammed to the brim and overflowing with strange adventures, dangers. It has a special kind of glamour such as only a handful of men have ever known. The bottom of the sea is truly the last land-mass frontier and for centuries has resisted all man's conquering efforts. There is more wealth buried beneath the sea than is in evidence in the world today. The history of man's life at sea, from the first hollowed log to the fifty-thousand-ton dreadnaught, is written below. The victories and defeats of nations are there in rotting, rusting hulks. It is the world's richest, greatest, and most carefully guarded graveyard for countless millions of unnamed things. Gross ugliness and delicate beauty go hand in hand down below and there is a teeming life that common man cannot even guess at.

On the bottom of the sea things happen to the diver that could not possibly happen anywhere else. I have had fish peer in at the face plate, mouths plastered tight against the glass like kids before a Christmas store window. They have gathered around and nibbled at my fingers and the brass fittings on the helmet while I worked. You would think it would be quiet down there, but it is not. A big fish shooting past makes a swish-swish-swishing sound with his tail. A six-foot halibut starts off with a rush from a pebbly bottom and sounds like a hot-rod taking the turn on a gravel road.

This noise is fine with me. After I acquired experience and confidence I was at my noisiest best. You see, I love to sing. I do not sing well but I do sing loud. The bottom of the sea is the one place where I can give out without fear of being thrown out of the joint or asked to move from the neighborhood. The brass confines of the helmet make the acoustics a hundred times clearer and richer than the shower or bathtub. I have been right in the middle of a song when a disgusted voice will say over the telephone, "Look, Virg, I don't mind working the telephone. I don't mind your cussing and I can even stand your bawling like a bull when something goes wrong, but—do I have to listen to that God-awful racket you're making now?"

Ballet dancing is another art at which I am a master under water. In roughly two hundred pounds of suit I am lightness and grace itself. I can stand on a rock, make a nimble leap and sail twenty feet to land feather light on another rock. Or I can, if the fancy strikes me, hover above the rock indefinitely, rise and lower at will. I can stand on bottom, and in one graceful spring soar to the top of a thirty-foot rock. I can step off the top and take five minutes to settle to the ocean's floor or I can stop halfway down and go back up. There is no need to creep carefully down and up the sides of the small ravines and canyons I find down there. It is simple to sail like Superman from side to side. It is all done with the chin valve. Keep it closed so the air builds up and the tendency soon is to float to the surface. Bump the valve, expelling air, and you sink. It's as simple as that.

Of course, I never go into these underwater acrobatics unless I am so deep the tenders can't see.

There is, however, one outstanding accomplishment I would be happy to display any time. I am sure I could jam the biggest theater in the land and stand the people for blocks. That is, a demonstration of feats of strength. Under water the most anemic peanut-breasted man is a Sampson, and a normally strong man can make all the physical culture ads ever written sound like gross understatements. A rock you can barely budge on land you can toss about one-handed down there. A ten-foot log a foot through you can juggle with almost the same ease Ted Williams does a baseball bat.

In diving, I also learned, your thinking of work must be revised in a number of ways. For instance, if you saw off a piling in the world of air, you must watch that it does not fall on your feet. Under water it is your face that may get in the way—the face plate could be smashed and you would be in trouble with the sea pouring in. The cut piling immediately shoots toward the surface, so do not get above it. On land, if you need a load of lumber a truck dumps it and that is that. Under water each piece must be weighted with iron to sink it to the job.

Time has no meaning down below. On my second dive I told the tender to let me know when I had been down thirty minutes. I would have sworn it was not more than ten when he called. This time lapse is understandable. First, you are busy keeping track of half a dozen things, any one of which can cause you serious trouble. Second, you are in a strange and fascinating world, in which every step may bring anything from a sunken wreck to an octopus or shark out of the gray distance.

Nothing happened during those early practice dives and I went blissfully along getting used to the suit and learning to handle myself under water. I gained confidence with every dive and I made a lot of dives in a few days. I would stay down an hour or so, come up and rest, and return to the bottom again. A half-dozen trips to bottom during a day was not unusual. I no longer went in head first. I floated now, and went down when ready, landing feather light and upright on bottom. My ascent was just as effortless. I gave up the life line, not through any sense of bravado but because pulling two hundred or so feet of air line and telephone line and fighting the push of the sea was hard enough.

When I was finally called to cut the concrete from the underwater passage to the ammunition room I was completely confident. I had not given a thought to what would happen when I pulled the trigger of a jackhammer and loosed a couple of hundred pounds of air pressure under water. I thought all hell had blown up and I was in the middle of it. Sound beat at me with giant fists and a white froth exploded before the face plate, completely blinding me. I dropped the hammer and stood there shaking and letting my heart settle back to place. That thin veneer of confidence was gone; for a moment near panic had claimed me. After a little I picked up the hammer and finished the job. It took forty minutes and I collected seventy-five dollars.

On the run back to Sitka I thought about this dive just completed and the sudden fright that had yelled through me the moment something had happened that I had not foreseen. I knew then, and was to realize more fully later, that this fright was a fine thing. Overconfidence leads to carelessness, and carelessness to disaster.

4

Death Waits Below

The luck that had accompanied me North still held. My next diving job enabled me to gain more of the skill I so desperately needed.

The job was at the Sitka Naval Base about a half mile from Sitka, across the bay. They had laid a water line, telephone cable, electric power lines and an oil or gas line from the mainland. Then they built a dock over the lines. That called for a diver on bottom to keep the lines clear as they drove pilings. For a month I walked about down there, catching pilings as they materialized out of the gloom. I would steer them onto bottom, making sure the lines were clear, yell into the telephone, "Hit it!" then walk away and sit down on a rock while the driver stomped the piling into the sea's bottom.

Then the drill barge caught fire and burned. It sank in the channel with a loss of almost two million dollars in machinery and two hundred cases of dynamite. The barge lay in eighty feet of water. This would be the deepest dive I had made to date. Machinery had to be cut loose, cables hooked on from cranes above and lifted out. The inside of the barge was a forest of charred timbers, broken pipes and torn sheet steel with razorlike edges. Something was bound to happen crawling about among that.

I expected the air line to get hung up, and it did, dozens of times. I was afraid I would tear the suit but surprisingly I did not. I had removed about half the machinery before anything happened. When it did, it was none of the things I had been fearing.

I stuck my head out a hole in the side of the barge one day and looked into the face of a big black eel not three feet away. He hung there as if suspended, looking at me, not at all surprised or frightened. He grinned, showing me a huge mouth, with rows of needle-sharp teeth. He did not move forward, and it was plain he had no intention of backing up. I backed up fast about ten feet, and just stood there. A minute later the man on the telephone said, "I thought you were coming up, Virg."

"There's an eel down here with other ideas," I said.

"Is that all?" he scoffed. "Listen, an eel is just an underwater snake. Kick him in the face and come on up."

"You never saw a snake like this," I said and described the eel.

"I thought you meant one of them little river kind," he said. "Don't do anything that will get him excited. Don't make any moves at him, Virg. He could rip you to ribbons, he could snap the air line in two, or even . . ."

"Will you shut up," I yelled. I was frightened enough without his making it worse. "You just keep the compressor running and stand by. I'm staying right here until he leaves."

I sat down on a length of pipe to wait and worry. This was my first experience with anything other than harmless fish and

I did not know what to do. "Suppose he comes in? Do I fight him?" I asked myself. "Should I try to bluff him out, then fight if I have to?" I had a knife that I had made with an eighteen-inch blade fastened in a scabbard to my lead belt. But I could not see myself doing much against his size and bullet speed. Anyway, that was a last resort. My greatest worry, at the moment, was my air line. It came through the same hole and his ugly snout was just three feet from it. One playful nip could sever it and I would be left here with the rest of the wreckage.

The tender asked, "Virg, how long can you stay down at eighty feet?"

"I don't know," I said. That was another worry and for all I knew it might be more dangerous than the eel.

Every few minutes I would cautiously peek out. He was still there in the same spot. "I've got all the time in the world," his attitude said. A couple of years went by.

The tender said, "Maybe that's his home and he's afraid to go in because you're there."

"That could be," I said. "But there is nothing I can do about it." I was afraid to move in any direction for fear it might attract his attention to the air line. So I sat and waited.

At such times your mind considers all sorts of possibilities, and regardless of how improbable they may seem normally, during the stress of that time they are very possible. I wondered how much gas we had for the compressor. Suppose we ran out? Suppose the compressor broke down? Suppose a williwaw struck (one of those sudden storms with hundred-mile-an-hour winds that boom out of the Aleutians without warning)? That forty-foot boat on the surface would never

live through it. Every one of those possibilities meant death
for me.

A couple of more years crawled away. I stuck my head out
again, jerked it back, and immediately stuck it out again.
There was no big grinning mouth, no malevolent look. No
eel! I went to the top fast.

The eel had held me on bottom more than an hour. Except
for my shredded nerves nothing had happened.

I dove the drill barge at least a dozen times more. I always
looked for my big grinning friend the moment I hit bottom
and the last thing before I left. I never saw him again.

By the time I had finished the job I was feeling confident at
eighty feet. This had been good experience, because the very
next dive took me deeper than I had ever dreamed I would go
—deeper, in fact, than many divers go in a lifetime of diving.

A Navy fighter plane ran out of gas a mile short of the base
and plunged into the sea. The pilot bailed out and, while
floating in his Mae West waiting rescue, took careful bearings
on his position. The Navy decided on one dive to try to recover the plane.

This would be in water two hundred feet deep and I would
have to use an underwater light. The sea would be squeezing
in dead earnest at this depth. The actual pressure on my body
would be slightly more than ninety tons, which the air in the
suit must counterbalance to keep me alive. I would be breathing air under more than a hundred pounds pure pressure. The
day before the dive I inspected minutely every inch of the suit
and air line, checked and double checked all connections.

The small boat we used was packed with naval personnel
when we pulled out into the sea. A young, sharp-looking lieutenant seemed to be in charge and he made a production of

the job with his strutting, unnecessary orders and brusque manners. He came up as I was getting into the suit, stopped spread-legged before me and ordered, "Take a good look around down there, Diver. This will be the only dive."

I tried to explain that we should not dive at the exact spot the plane hit the water. We should figure the angle it struck and try to judge the direction it took after that, since a plane, like a bullet, will not sink on a straight line.

"Look, mister," he said, "do you want to make this dive or not?"

"Of course," I said.

"Then get at it."

They had rigged a makeshift diving platform to take me down. (The Navy always dives from platforms). I wanted to go down as I always had, so if anything went wrong I could stop anywhere and come back up. But the lieutenant told me with flat authority, "You dive from that, mister, or you don't dive!"

A sailor set on the helmet, put the underwater light in my hand and I stepped onto the platform. Two sailors swung the boom over and lowered me into the slate-gray sea. They held the platform at chest depth while I adjusted the air. Then I said, "Ready to dive!" and the platform went down. The water turned steadily darker as the depth increased.

I had tied strings onto the air line every twenty feet and the sailor on the telephone tolled off the footage steadily. "Eighty —one hundred—one-twenty—one-forty . . ." I looked up. The surface light was a mere shading of lighter dark far above.

Pressure hit me with frightening suddenness, clamping onto my legs and creeping upward into my chest. I turned on more air and the pressure slunk away. The air roaring into the hel-

met made the sailor's voice hollow and far away. "One-sixty
—one-eighty . . ." The platform stopped with a jar.

"Okay. On bottom!" I said in the high, squeaky voice great
depths give because of pressure on the vocal cords.

I stepped off the platform and sank a foot into soft mud. It
was dead black. I switched on the underwater light and it
punched a pale shaft that reached barely ten feet. I moved off,
bending forward against the pull of unseen currents and the
great weight of the sea. After a short distance I stopped and
swung the light about, and found nothing.

There was something about a plane. . . . At two hundred
feet pressure has a definite effect on the mind. Your reason for
being down is hazy and you forget easily. Even when you're
conscious of the reason, you don't care if you do anything
about it or not. I had the strangest feeling I wanted to sit
down on a rock and just stay there. On shallow dives I had
taught myself to judge time fairly well. Now I did not know
if I had been down ten minutes or an hour, and I did not care.
The voice from the surface kept repeating in the earphones,
"You find the plane yet, Diver? You been down almost fifteen
minutes."

I used the diving platform as a hub and moved off in another direction poking holes in the liquid blackness around
me. I seemed to have a thousand pounds on my shoulders; my
legs shook and breathing was a wracking effort. I returned to
the platform and leaned against it. The voice in the earphones
said, "You've been down twenty-five minutes. You find anything yet, Diver?"

"No," I said. "Not yet." I slogged off into the blackness
again. Fish streaked through the light beam and in that brief

instant they seemed different from those nearer the surface—much uglier.

It seemed to me I returned to the platform several times more, rested briefly, then moved off in a different direction each time. I may have passed within three or four feet of the plane half a dozen times. When I returned to the platform the last time the voice in the earphones said, "You've been down forty-five minutes. You find the plane yet?"

Forty-five minutes, I thought vaguely. That was my limit at this depth. But he was crazy. I had only made two—or was it three?—trips out from the platform. Fifteen minutes, maybe. There was a lot of bottom I had not covered.

The voice repeated, "Did you find the plane?"

The plane, I thought, yeah, the plane. "No," I said. "No plane."

"You had better come up. You've been down long enough."

"Go up? But I haven't found the plane."

"You on the platform, Diver?" the voice asked. "We're bringing you up."

I stood there leaning against the platform, dimly thinking of the plane, thinking of going up. The voice said again, "Diver, are you on the platform?"

I stepped on the platform and took hold of the cables. "Okay," I said. "Okay, haul away."

The platform rose out of the silt toward the distant unseen surface. Going up took almost two hours as I had to stop at intervals to let the gas bubbles escape from my blood stream to avoid the dreaded bends.

I had gone to two hundred feet and the fact I was still alive was proof I had made no mistakes. But I was unhappy over the dive. I felt it could have been successful if the lieutenant had listened to reason. I do not know what I would have done if he had been in charge on the dive I made for the Army later.

In trying to lift a load from a barge, the operator of a seventy-ton caterpillar crane had swung the boom out too far, losing his leverage, and when the weight of the load hit the cables the crane toppled off the dock into the sea.

It lay in forty feet of water, the top end of the boom wedged against the face of the dock. When I arrived, a pair of steel cables had been secured to the dock's edge and hung in the water. They wanted me to go below and fasten them about the cab of the crane. In a week or so, when they had assembled another pair of cranes they were now working on, they would lift this one.

It looked like an easy hundred dollars. It was not deep and the simplest operation possible. There was plenty of help. Half a dozen soldiers were crowded on the work boat with me and a couple hundred more lounged on the dock, watching. The young fellow on the telephone and I kidded each other as I dressed.

"That is some man-from-Mars get-up, mac," he said.

"Latest thing in sport clothes," I said. "The hat's guaranteed not to leak or wrinkle and the shoes not to wear out."

"I can believe that," he said.

I pulled out a foot of slack at my belly and said, "It won't need much alteration either. You'll be the best-dressed man in the joint when you step out in this."

"Is that a fact?"

"Sure thing," I said. "You're top man."

"I could go for that. Look, mac, when you finish this job

how about us going in someplace where it is nice and shallow and let me try it on?"

"You want to go down?"

"I would like to if it is nice and shallow."

"Then I'd better finish this job," I said. They set on the helmet and I jumped in immediately.

The bottom was rock and sand; the water was clear. The crane lay tipped half on its side, one corner buried in the bottom.

I climbed the side of the cab with the first cable, looped it over, brought it down the side and wedged the hook under the edge. Then I crawled under the tilted side to pull it through.

The hook was a couple of feet beyond my reaching fingers and I clawed and shoved rocks aside, inching forward until I had it. I pulled the cable through and began backing out. While still half under the crane I felt it suddenly shift and roll sluggishly above me. I jerked to my knees to get out quick and was yanked up short by the air line. As I had walked around and crawled under the cab, the air line had slipped under the tilted edge. My digging, or some other disturbance, had upset a delicate balance, causing it to tilt farther, bringing the edge of the cab down on the air line and wedging it tight. By some freak of luck it was not pinched shut and air still came through. But I could not move forward to reach the wedged spot or backward to clear the cab. I was trapped under seventy tons of crane!

I have read of people who passed through a life-or-death experience saying that they had been so frightened they had passed beyond fear to fatalistic calm.

That happened to me. After the first terrified moment I

crouched there on all fours and my thinking seemed clearer, more deliberate than it had ever been. Fear was gone, or at least for the moment had been forced into the background.

I seemed to be two people. One was trapped under a crane, the other stood to one side, calmly impersonal, considered the plight of the trapped man and coolly gauged his chances for survival. "He is in a mighty tough spot," this second man said. "Maybe he will get out, maybe he won't. He is going to have to do something in a hurry and it will have to be the right thing the first time. He will never get a second chance."

The trapped man thought, "The men on top can't help me. The only possible help I can get is from the two cranes that will not be assembled for another week. And I can't stay trapped down here for a week.

"If I get out I will have to do it on my own and there isn't much time. The crane may shift again any moment and this time I will be smashed to jelly. The first thing is to get from under the crane. That means cutting the air line. I can do that and not drown—the automatic valve in the helmet will close, keeping out the sea." Without fresh air I was sure I could live five or six minutes. I would be free of the crane but still forty feet from the surface. Here those experimental dives, that trial-and-error knowledge of the suit I had acquired, began to pay off in big fat dividends. Enough air in the suit floated me. But I would not have that air; this and the weight of the suit would hold me on bottom. Suppose I dropped some weight to make up for the air I would not have? I could shuck the lead belt and shoes thus getting rid of some one-hundred-twenty pounds. There would still be almost three hundred pounds of man and suit to float up. Would the air left in the suit do that? There was only one way to find out.

I planned it all before I told the man on the telephone what had happened and how I meant to get out.

"After I cut the air line," I told him, "I'll have to work fast. I will have to cut the air line loose from the crane so you can pull it up, take off my shoes and lead belt, float to the surface and get the helmet off in less than six minutes."

"You're sure you can float up?" he asked anxiously.

"I'm sure," I said. "But you have got to get a boat and be right over the spot where I'll surface. See where my bubbles are coming up now and get a boat right there. And remember —you have to catch me the first grab. There won't be enough air in the suit to float me. I'll just bob to the surface and sink again. If I do, I'm a goner. Remember—you have got to catch me with the first grab! There won't be a second chance!"

"Okay," came the answer. "Give us time to get the boat. I'll let you know when. Don't cut that air line yet."

While I waited, crouched on hands and knees I reviewed each step. I dreaded most cutting the air line. Once divorced from that, I had cut my life to minutes.

Finally the tender's voice said, "All set up here! We've got a rowboat over the spot your bubbles are coming up. Come ahead, mac! We're waiting."

"Be there in a minute!" I twisted the knife from the scabbard, breathed a little prayer and slashed at the tough hose. The second cut parted it with a burst of bubbles.

I crawled out, rounded the cab, and cut the hose loose from the crane. Then I knelt and began working frantically at the buckles of my shoes.

I kicked off one but the second resisted all efforts. Then I discovered I had not loosened the thong from the metal loop. Seconds later, it was off. I unbuckled the lead belt, slipped the left strap—the right. This was the moment I was still worried about. The instant I dropped the belt I soared smoothly upward. I looked up and the bottom of the rowboat was rushing at me. I broke the surface not three feet away, hands clamped onto me and hauled me into the boat. They unscrewed the helmet and lifted it off. The young tender said in all seriousness, "I just went out of the diving business, mac."

I breathed the wonderful air, blinked at the wonderful sun and smiled at the wonderful men. "When we finish this job," I said, "we're all going to have a drink on the diver."

Later, I got a spare belt, fastened the air line to the helmet again, returned to bottom, put on my shoes and finished the job in a few minutes.

One of the best protections a diver can have is a good man on the opposite end of the telephone line.

Consider the case of the burned fish dock. The New England Fish Company dock had burned and they built a new one. But a number of old pilings still thrust up from bottom, presenting a menace to navigation. They wanted me to blow them off flush with bottom. To do this you fasten four or five dynamite sticks around the piling, then touch it off with an electric coil from the surface.

The only helper I could get was a nineteen-year-old school kid on vacation. To make matters worse, a broken oil line had spilled thousands of barrels of black oil across the surface of the bay. That would cut visibility to almost nothing.

We anchored over the spot where the old dock had been, and I got into the suit. The kid looked at the lead shoes, breastplate, helmet and lead belt. He said doubtfully, "Virg, how will I ever haul you up in all that gear?"

"I'll inflate the suit and float up," I told him.

"You kidding?"

"I'll float. Don't worry."

"But the life line—I always thought divers used a life line."

"I used to," I explained. "But it's easier to blow myself to the surface. You just worry about that telephone and air line and keep the compressor running."

I showed him how the compressor worked, told him to watch the poundage, then had him put on the helmet and lock it. I was ready to dive. The kid stirred the oil about, making a hole to dive through. I picked up three strings of dynamite sticks, shuffled to the rail and jumped into the hole.

Forty feet down, the Alaskan silt billowed like smoke around the face plate. The oil on the surface had cut the visibility to about three feet. I knew I stood in the middle of a field of broken pilings but I had to grope for each one, then try to guess its height by reaching high as I could. I meant to blow only those that thrust high enough to be a menace at low water. I draped the three strings around pilings and, carrying a long wire from each, went to the surface and climbed the diving ladder to avoid the charge's concussion. It is terrific under water.

The kid hooked the wires to the coil and set them off. There was a solid *whoomp*, like a deep-sea belch, then a boil of dirty water. An instant later a piling bobbed up, accompanied by a half-dozen dead fish.

That first explosion raised a cloud of silt which, added to the oil, cut all light from the bottom. Forty feet down, where I worked the rest of the day, I could not see my hand before the face plate. Strangely, that first piling was the only one that floated.

On the way down the second day I passed the butt of a

big piling thrusting toward the surface. It lay cradled across the bracing, and the fact that it had not risen told me this wood was lead-heavy with creosote and but for the braces would sink.

I went on down, had blown some half-dozen sticks and was again on bottom groping toward another, when the air line jerked taut.

I yelled, "Give me more line!" and pulled. The line stayed taut.

"You've got plenty of line," the kid said. "Just pull."

I knew then that I was hung up and began groping my way back along the air line hunting the spot. I found that the big piling had become dislodged and slid off the bracing. It had sunk to bottom, coming to rest on top of the air line, burying it a foot in the silt.

I got my arms around the butt and tried to lift it. It was solid as Gibraltar. I straightened, and that moment felt the water climbing inside the suit. The thing I had always feared most had happened! In lifting, I had snagged the suit on a nail, knot or sliver, and the sea was pouring in. In a matter of seconds the water would be in the helmet.

The sudden, clamming feel of the sea is a terrifying thing. My first thought was to inflate and shoot to the surface, but the piling prevented that. I felt about, found the hole, a tear about two inches long just below the breastplate. I pinched it shut and felt the water stop, waist high in the suit.

For a little while I stood there getting my panic under control; then I called the kid. "I'm having a little trouble," I said, "and you've got to help me. A piling has my air line pinned down and there is a rip in the suit. The water is getting inside with me. . . ."

"My God!" he yelled. "You'll drown. You'll drown! What'll I do?"

"Do exactly as I tell you," I said. "Listen, I won't drown. The air pressure inside the helmet will keep the water below my nose. But tie the saw to a line and send it down so I can cut the piling in two."

I stood in the pitch-darkness, pinching the rip together, waiting. The water in the suit was no higher. I felt the steady tug of the current as the tide ran and heard the *tunk-tunk-tunk* of the compressor like a small reassuring voice in the helmet. I tipped my head back, looking up, waiting for the saw.

It took shape a foot above my head. I reached for it, practically had it, when the current swept it away. I waited again.

Then suddenly, "I can't get it down to you. The God-damned current keeps swinging it away. But don't you worry. I'll get you out of there, Virg."

"Listen," I said, "just don't get excited. You didn't have a weight on the saw. Tie a shackle to it and let it down again."

There was no answer, and I repeated it. Still no answer, and I yelled, "Hey, kid, do you hear me?"

The phone was dead. Probably a broken connection, but he would never know that. Now I could not tell him what to do: I stood there for a little, waiting, hoping he would lower the saw again. Then I knew it was not coming. I tried to imagine what he was doing. Probably yelling into the telephone, wondering why I did not answer.

I tried pulling one-handed on the air line thinking I might seesaw it to the end of the piling and loosen it. A vice could not have held it tighter. The silt had to be dug away to give it play. Even then it might still be too tight but there was nothing else I could do. I got down on my knees and began clawing one-handed. It was immediately apparent this was a two-handed job. I straightened and let go of the rip and felt the water begin rising. It climbed swiftly to my chest, my shoulders. Then it was in the helmet. The air pressure in the helmet stopped it at my chin. The protective padding of air was gone from the suit and the sea's pressure was bending my ribs.

I got down on my knees again and began scooping out silt with both hands.

Try squatting on your knees and digging without looking down or bending your head. That was the way I worked. If I looked down, the water in the helmet covered my nose and mouth.

I dug frantically, like a dog at a gopher hole, first on one side of the piling then the other. I stood up, my heart in my mouth, and began seesawing.

It worked! I made maybe a foot and was stuck again, but that was the longest twelve inches in the world.

I jammed my fingers into sharp-edged rocks, old rusty tin cans, bottles; I felt the bite of salt water in torn flesh, but that did not matter. I was making headway.

After an eternity I stood up for the last time and seesawed the line free of the butt of the piling. I followed it back until it rose straight up. Forty feet above was the boat.

There the second problem presented itself. Normally I would float up. Now water filled all the air space in the suit. There was only one thing to do—climb the air line.

I always tell a new tender to be sure to take a couple of good turns around something solid with the air line, so it will not all run out and perhaps tip over the compressor. I made a test pull. I pulled harder—harder. I put my full weight on it and began to climb. I don't know how I made those forty feet, or why the air line did not break, or the loose turns the kid had taken about a cleat slip.

The first thing I noticed was that there was no kid on deck. The telephone was lying on the coil of air line. So it had not gone dead. The little louse had panicked, run out on me!

I got the face plate open and sat there on the rail staring up at the bright sun and tasting the fresh air. Oh, you can taste it, and no honey is sweeter. The water level slowly dropped in the suit as it ran out the tear down onto the deck. My fingers were torn and bleeding. There was not a whole nail left on either hand. Then I saw the kid. He was on the dock talking with the operator of a clam-shell dredge.

I heard his sudden yell when he spotted me, and I heard the splash of oars as he rowed out, but I did not look up. "Let him come aboard," I thought. "Let him get close enough so I can get my hands on him! Just let him come!"

He popped over the side. "Virg! You made it." He flopped down weakly on the edge of the boat. "Man, was I scared."

"No thanks to you," I snapped. "You ran out on me."

"Ran out!" he cried aghast. "I went after that clam shell. I wanted them to let it down right over you and lift you out, but they wouldn't do it."

"Good thing they wouldn't," I snarled. "That clam shell would have smashed me flat if it had hit me. And if they had got hold of me they'd have pulled me in two."

"That's what the fellow said, but he was going to try to lift the piling off you. I was going to ride the bucket down and steer it over the piling. I'd have done it if it killed me. I said I would get you out, Virg."

It might have worked, but he would have been taking an awful chance riding the bucket into forty feet of black, ice-cold water. I thought of that fine, dangerous gesture he had been about to make to rescue me, and I was ashamed of my temper.

That evening I sat alone in the galley patching the suit. Through the open door I could see the days were lengthening. Light still touched the high snow peaks ringing the bay, but down here dusk lay over land and sea. Gulls had settled for the night along the dock edge and on the building ridges. The silhouettes of boats moved into and out of the harbor. Feet made a steady pacing along the dock and an occasional voice rang out. I thought of today's close shave, even closer, in some ways, than the experience with the overturned crane. "You came within a hair of getting killed," I told myself.

But, strangely, this near escape seemed to have happened to someone else in another world. I knew now there would be other close ones. It was impossible to continue in this business without them. Whether you are ten feet down or two hundred, there is no real protection.

I had learned something new about the way a diver thinks. You take your danger where you find it and you take it in stride. You have conditioned your mind to the risks involved. It is the same principle that makes you try to beat the yellow light before it turns red, or dodge the screwball driver when you cross the street. Only, the diver's risks seem greater.

Why did I stay with it? There was the money I was sending home at regular intervals now. That stake Wilma and I had wanted must be getting pretty big. But there were other reasons. The same reasons that had made me run away from home as a kid, that had me prospecting in the Salmon River

Country, and wanting to become a cowboy, that had me rambling the country for years as a carnival fighter. The love of adventuring, of seeing new sights, new lands. And I had found the most amazing place known to man to adventure in, the oldest, newest frontier on earth—the bottom of the sea.

A storm poured out of the Aleutians and for three days and nights it pounded at the land and installations. When it was over the Navy was afraid the power and telephone lines that stretched from the mainland to the base in the bay might have been washed together. I was hired to walk the half mile of the bay's floor and separate the lines fifty feet.

I began at the Sitka side with the tender following on the surface. I would pick up the power line, carry it to one side, lay it down, walk down it until it came close to the telephone line, lift it and carry it over again. The bottom was sandy and tipped gently down going steadily deeper. The water was very clear.

I was somewhere near the middle of the bay in well over a hundred feet, lifting, carrying, laying down, walking again. The constant repetition, the sameness of the bottom formation and vegetation were making the job monotonous. Then the next minute all that was changed. I stopped short at what I beheld. Unable to believe what I was seeing, I wondered if the distortion of the depths or the oxygen pressure was doing things to my mind and eyes.

Rising out of the deeper, gray-green gloom ahead were the sterns of two sailing ships. They lay about fifty feet apart, tipped partially on their sides, tilting away from each other. The mast on one was broken. The other's stretched upward to disappear into the water. The decks were thickly coated with kelp, seaweed and barnacles. Long kelp streamers clung to the masts, waving lazily to the pull of a current. The lines I had been following ran exactly between the two ships.

My heart pounding with excitement I moved to the low rail of the nearest and looked onto the sloping deck. There was the black opening of a doorway leading below. Everything was buried deep under barnacles and silt. I lifted a lead foot, kicked the side of the ship and the planking caved through. I took hold of the high wooden rail, pulled, and a four-foot section fell out, lifting a cloud of silt. Old—years and years old.

I stepped through and moved gingerly onto the sloping deck. A little way off lay a ship's bell, beyond that a pair of blocks, vague outlines beneath the silt. Almost at my feet was a gun with a broken stock and a barrel about four feet long. Around the deck at spaced intervals were ragged holes eight to ten feet square. I could guess these holes had once held muzzle-loading cannon and the years and rotting wood and their great weight had finally broken them through into the hold.

I crept along the deck and looked into the nearest hole but could see nothing through the inner blackness. The temptation to go down inside was tremendous but common sense said I might dislodge something that would bring the whole rotten deck down upon me. And then I was remembering my friend the eel and another I had not yet met, the octopus. Old wrecks, I had heard, were his favorite haunt.

I stood there thinking of these two old ships and the people who had probably been aboard and what could have happened. There were no signs of a battle, no evidence that they had crashed something and sunk. There were no skeletons on deck or lying about on the floor of the sea. Two ships without a soul aboard either one? Ghost ships? That was highly unlikely. Were the holds filled with skeletons? If so, why? Had there been mutiny aboard and holes chopped in the bottoms so they would sink? It would be a million to one chance of that happening to two ships together. But it was a million to one that I had found them. The sea is full of unsolved mysteries and this was my first. I dropped a hundred years standing there, speculating. I was again in an era of muzzle-loading guns, of grotesque iron cannons and flashing cutlasses. I was listening to a strange tongue, seeing strange men, hearing the snap and crack of canvas being hit by the wind. Then a disgustingly blunt but familiar voice said, "Hey, what's wrong down there? You ain't moved in twenty minutes."

"Nothing wrong," I snapped. I looked at the old bell, I would have liked to take that up with me but I was afraid to cross the deck for it. I pried the broken musket from the deck at my feet and carried it back onto the floor of the sea with me. Then I went on with my twentieth-century job of carrying a power line that furnished electricity for a complete naval base.

People to whom I showed the old gun identified it as an ancient Russian piece. The barrel was octagonal and almost an inch thick. It had taken a real man to lift and fire it. I tried to raise some stories on the two ships, but the closest I came was that a hundred years ago the Russian traders at Fort Archangel Gabriel had engaged in a battle with the natives. The natives had won, driving the traders away and burning their headquarters. Two years later the Russians returned, and in the ensuing battle the natives were driven into the hills. No report mentioned anything about lost ships. But maybe these two had been there, lying at anchor, and the natives had slipped aboard at night, cut them loose and hacked holes in the bottoms so they would drift off and sink—maybe.

I have often thought of going back. There are ways of getting below decks. A little dynamite to blow the deck away, a small crane and line to clear wreckage. Who can say what you might find? But I will never go back. Whatever story is buried among the barnacles, old cannon and rotting timbers, is well buried and has been for many, many years. Maybe it should be left that way.

5

I Meet the Fish Pirates

The Navy brought several of their own divers into Sitka. From then on I got no more dives from the armed forces. This cut my paydays to an alarming low. I was wondering which way to turn, when the salmon canneries in Prince William Sound approached me with offers to dive for them. I was to inspect and repair the underwater sections of their fish traps. They would supply me a boat, gas, oil and grub and guarantee me some thirty dives a season. So, I found myself with a thirty-foot boat, the Western Fisheries *Number 9*, and the diving gear set up on deck, ready to take off across the Sound's blue water.

Prince William Sound is more than 7500 square miles of sea cupped in a giant bowl that is ringed by snow-capped mountains and dozens of glaciers. There were more than thirty traps scattered about this vast area. Some were as much as a day's run by boat apart. This would be far different from operating about the small bay at Sitka. Now I must navigate by charts.

I knew nothing of charts, and I had not the vaguest idea

as to the locations of the traps. So that night, carrying my new charts, I went aboard Eric Johnson's tender to ask his help. Eric was a grizzled, wrinkled old skipper, the kind you see in pictures with a floppy sou'wester hat, rubber boots and slicker. His favorite saying was, "I know every point, rock and grain of sand from here to Valdez and back."

I found him in the galley drinking coffee. He listened to my tale of woe, then shoved the coffee cup aside, saying, "You take it easy. I fix you right up."

He spread my charts on the galley table and began making crosses at each trap's location and penciling in the trap's name. He added bits of information as he worked, "Now this is a Western Fisheries trap. Wind hits hard here and kicks up big waves. If you pull in behind the trap you won't get the boat stove in slamming against the logs when it's rough. This is a New England trap. It's got a bad tide run you have to watch. This is an Ellamar trap. It's got a bad tide run, too, and the wind comes hard around that point. Early morning will be the best time to dive that trap." He added bits of information with every trap. I could not remember half that he told me. He marked dangerous rocks, shallows and points. He pointed out the good passages and the bad, and showed me how to spot them. In the simplest language possible he taught me how to lay out and follow a course, how to fit the line of the chart with the coast I was passing.

He warned me against anchoring long in shallow bays when the tide was in. "When it goes out maybe you find yourself in the mud," he said. "Always remember, figure the tide when you come to anchor." He made a special point of telling me about the windstorms. They could come up out of a bright, quiet day, he explained, and in five minutes a smooth sea would be churned into ten-foot waves. "Your little boat can't take those seas. You keep an eye out all the time for protected bays, points and islands to get behind. When you see white water ahead run for cover. You had better get a pair of binoculars so you're sure you know what you're seeing. And another thing—watch your tide runs. Figure to go with the tide, instead of bucking it. You can save fuel and time." Finally he stopped and scratched his gray head. "That's some of it. It won't help to tell you more now. You will have to learn the rest as you go along. Just remember, if you are careful and lucky, you will be all right."

I returned to my boat with a new respect for Eric. There was thirty years of hard-earned knowledge behind those calm blue eyes. I was convinced if anyone knew every point, rock and grain of sand between Cordova and Valdez it must be Eric. I could guess how I must appear to such an old salt in my little thirty-footer. A green Idaho boy, who, until a few months ago, had never been in anything larger than a rowboat on a mountain lake. For a moment my own audacity overwhelmed me. But, I consoled myself, until I came North I had never seen a diving suit. Now I was a diver. I would learn this navigation, too.

That first trip around the Sound was brutally rough for a beginner and only luck and Eric's advice brought me through. I missed traps and had to double back. A dozen times I scraped hidden rocks, or suddenly found myself in a nest of them threading my way out while I held my breath, fearing every second to hear the crunch of the bow caving in. Once I took a wrong channel, though it was plainly marked "bad" on the chart. I ran aground and sat on the mud six hours waiting for the tide to float me. I ducked one wind-

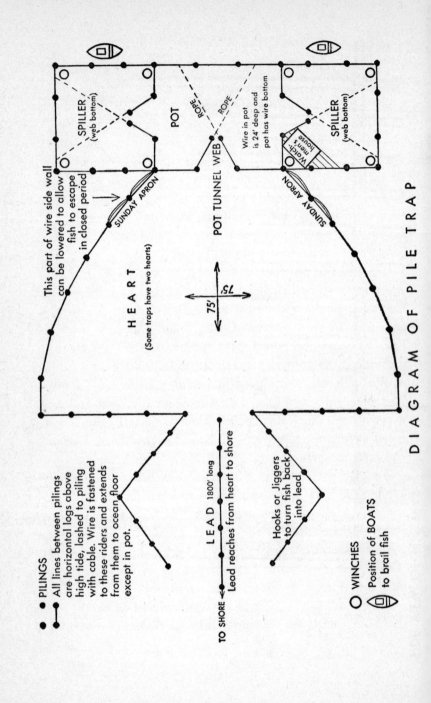

DIAGRAM OF PILE TRAP

PILINGS

All lines between pilings are horizontal logs above high tide, lashed to piling with cable. Wire is fastened to these riders and extends from them to ocean floor except in pot.

This part of wire side wall can be lowered to allow fish to escape in closed period

SPILLER (web bottom)

POT

ROPE

ROPE

Wire in pot is 24' deep and pot has wire bottom

SPILLER (web bottom)

Watch men's house

SUNDAY APRON

POT TUNNEL WEB

SUNDAY APRON

HEART (Some traps have two hearts)

75'

LEAD 1800' long

Lead reaches from heart to shore

TO SHORE

Hooks or Jiggers to turn fish back into lead

WINCHES

Position of BOATS to brail fish

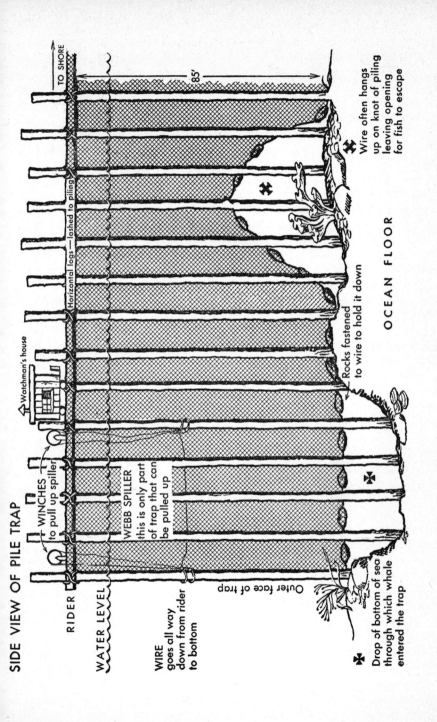

SIDE VIEW OF PILE TRAP

TO SHORE

Horizontal logs—lashed to piling

85'

Watchman's house

WINCHES to pull up spiller

WEBB SPILLER
this is only part of trap that can be pulled up

RIDER

WATER LEVEL

WIRE goes all way down from rider to bottom

Outer face of trap

OCEAN FLOOR

Wire often hangs up on knot of piling leaving opening for fish to escape

Rocks fastened to wire to hold it down

✠

Drop of bottom of sea through which whale entered the trap

storm, then became careless and was caught on the fringe of another where I was tossed about like a cork for half an hour until I staggered behind a point. But I found every trap and at each made the first inspection dive.

A fish trap, I discovered, is an ingeniously devised enclosure completely and tightly fenced in with chicken wire. It resembles an enormous mousetrap or the fun house in an amusement park. From shore, a chicken-wire fence stretches out to sea as much as a half or three-quarters of a mile to the trap. This drift fence is called the "lead." Salmon traveling up the coast, hunting a spawning stream, hit the lead, follow it out, looking for a way around, and are led into an enormous corral—the "jigger."

The jigger has a mousetrap opening at the far end that tempts Mr. Salmon. He dashes through, expecting the open sea, and finds himself in another corral slightly smaller than the first—the "heart." He discovers another opening at the far end of the heart and shoots happily through—into the "pot." From the pot another opening funnels him into the smallest enclosure of all, where he finds thousands of other salmon literally crawling over each other. This is the "spiller." From here there is no escape except by "brailer," the gigantic dip net operated from the boom of the cannery tender. The spiller has one special distinction—its sides and bottom are made of rope netting. When the tender arrives to empty the trap the net is pulled up, forcing the salmon to the top where the brail can scoop them out and into the hold of the boat a thousand at a time.

A fish trap will hold from fifty to seventy thousand fish and some traps have caught as many as a million in a single season.

At each trap the watchmen acted as my tenders. I would begin by inspecting the lead, then completely circle each compartment to make sure the wire was down clear to bottom all around. It was not unusual to find a "hold-up" on these first dives. A hold-up is a spot where the wire has hung up on a knot, nail or sliver on the piling as it was let down, thus leaving a hole underneath for fish to escape.

The water was not as cold as I had expected, due to the Japanese Current which swings in close to shore. Old-timers have put it at around thirty-eight degrees. But this could not affect me. The protective padding of air in the suit was always the same temperature as that on the surface. This insulated me against cold. If the day was seventy, I was seventy in the suit regardless of water temperature.

At the end of the first round of inspection dives I returned to Cordova feeling very much a sailor. As I passed Eric's tender he stepped on deck and waved. I leaned out the window and gave him the fighter's victory salute.

There was always work at some trap those first weeks. The canneries were rushing to get their traps in before season opened, so I was constantly on the go repairing and inspecting. In time I came to know the sound, not as well as Eric, but well enough to make the circuit without consulting the charts more than a dozen times.

Of all the people I met on that job, the most fascinating was that legendary character, the Alaskan fish pirate.

It is impossible to spend any time along the Alaskan coast and not hear amazing stories of his raids on the canneries' fish traps. In the countless places where fishermen gather, in bars, hotel lobbies, pool halls, on boats, pirating held a high priority over any other conversation.

I heard of the pirate who makes the rounds of the traps in the Sound each spring, lining up watchmen to help him steal from the traps. With each watchman he leaves a walkie-talkie so they can contact him when the trap is full and the coast is clear.

Another pirate has been known to sail past a trap in broad daylight when the cannery tender was there, then hoist the Jolly Roger in a thumb-to-nose gesture.

There is the pirate who makes a practice in any public argument of upholding the cannery from which he steals— "Don't you talk about that cannery. They built my home for me!" And he points to a palatial-like house in the hills above Ketchikan.

I have heard of the pirate who began operations in 1940 with an old broken-down hulk he resurrected off the beach. He equipped it with a conglomeration of gear donated by other fishermen. Today he owns two fine boats that he leases to the canneries, a big home in the States, and a legitimate marine business.

"Not that fish pirating ain't legitimate," the boys point out.

I met a cannery owner that everyone insists got his start pirating fish. Now that he owns a cannery, he fights his former allies with all an owner's zeal.

Fish pirating, I soon discovered, is a flourishing, recognized business. This amazing condition is brought about by the fish traps and by the fishermen's attitude toward them.

The traps are owned by the canneries and the same sites are leased to them year after year by the War Department, which is responsible for seeing that traps do not obstruct navigation. There was a time when a cannery could put in a trap wherever it chose. Now all sites are designated by the U. S. Fish and Wildlife Service. The canneries operate on the assumption that the fish caught in the traps are theirs to dispose of as they see fit.

The Alaskans disagree. They believe in another law, the White Act, which forbids the granting of exclusive fishing rights to any individual or group. Therefore they disapprove of the fish traps and in 1946 they registered their disapproval by voting them out eight to one. Being a territory their vote means nothing and Uncle Sam has not seen fit to help them yet, but the fish pirates have.

On the day the season opens pirates are combing the sea, sneaking on traps in the dead of night, in fog, storms and even broad daylight, giving the canneries unwanted help in gathering the Silver Harvest. The incidents that occur are told and retold by cannery workers, seiners and trap watchmen. Two in particular I heard again and again that first season I dove.

It seemed that a cannery owner became suspicious when one of his traps continued to have small catches. One night in a speedboat he slipped up silently to the trap and caught a pirate in the act of robbing it. The watchman, a nineteen-year-old kid, was helping. The pirate jumped aboard his boat, started the engine and rammed it in gear. But nothing happened. He had forgotten to untie his boat from the trap and he hung there just grinding away. The watchman became excited and ran off the logs into the trap. The owner hauled him out and stood there roaring with laughter. The pirate, seeing nothing funny, dashed aft, slashed the rope with a knife and took off full tilt.

Most workmen enjoy seeing the boss taken for a ride, and this second story delighted the cannery workers down to the cockles of their hearts. A seiner with an old beat-up boat came into the cannery day after day with staggering loads of fish. The amazing contradiction was that he worked alone, which no man can do, his equipment was worn out, and his seine holey. It was so rotten that straining water would have torn it in two. Everyone knew he was pirating and guessed the trap watchmen were helping him load. Finally the cannery superintendent accused him of it.

"Me, pirate!" the man said righteously. "I'll show you where I seined these fish any time."

The superintendent hopped aboard. "We'll go right now!" he announced with the air of a man who has sprung a neat trap.

A few hours later the old boat staggered back, decks almost awash with her load of fish. The superintendent was screaming. "You damn crook! You stole those fish out of our nearest trap. There wasn't time to seine a load, even if you could. There ain't but one trap in miles. Besides, this even looks like a trap-caught load. Look at them—there's five or six different kinds of fish—everything that gets into a trap. A seined load only catches one kind and you know it."

"I agreed to show you where I seined these," the fisherman said patiently. "If you want to sleep all the way out and back, that's your problem."

"You slipped me a mickey," the superintendent raged. "I should have known there was something phony when you offered me a drink."

"If you don't want the fish . . ." The pirate said with dignity.

"Oh, we'll take the fish. But damn you! leave our traps alone."

Soon I began meeting this hardy fraternity. It was logical that I would. I dove for half a dozen canneries and inspected every trap in the Sound. I learned an amazing number of things and some of my experiences could have happened only on a new frontier like Alaska.

My own pirate education began one sunny afternoon while I sat against the cannery buildings between dives enjoying the unusual warmth. The sea lay bright and flat across the bay. A row of seagulls squatted along the cannery ridge. Others waddled across the dock near me. A cloud of them boiled noisily over the water where the offal chute emptied into the bay. Not a hundred feet off, a stream from a mile-high glacier charged down the mountain and plunged into the sea. Over at the conveyor three men leisurely pitched fish from the hold of a boat onto the traveling belt. The salmon flashed silvery in the sunlight.

The cannery superintendent wandered along the dock, stopped and looked down at the three men. Suddenly he blew this calm day to bits. "Damn you!" he shouted. "You stole those fish out of one of our traps and I know it."

The biggest of the three fishermen, a young fellow wearing a baseball cap and sporting a face-full of black whiskers, leaned on his pew and said in an aggrieved voice, "Aw now, Nick! What are you talking about?"

"You know damn well what I'm talking about! This is the last time I'm going to tell you. Keep away from our traps. Understand? Keep away!"

"If you don't want the fish, there's half a dozen other canneries we can go to," Whiskers said calmly. "Just say the word."

The superintendent clenched his fists. "Oh, I'll take your fish this time. But it's the last," he warned. "Tomorrow I'm putting rifles aboard every trap, with orders to sink your damn tub if it even comes in range."

"I can see your point," Whiskers said sympathetically. "But you're getting steamed up at the wrong people. We're just seiners that have been lucky at making good hauls." He smiled at the apoplectic superintendent. "This is our third good haul in a week. I figure we must have about ten thousand here, don't you?"

The superintendent glared at them, seeming on the verge of jumping into the boat to wreak havoc. Then he said in an ominous voice, "Just remember what I said about those rifles!" With that he swung on his heel and stalked away. The three young fellows looked at each other, then burst out laughing.

Their boat was plainly a seiner with all a seiner's gear. She was a nice job, around fifty feet, with a black hull and gray superstructure. She was built to carry a heavy load of fish.

A few days later I pulled into a trap for an inspection dive. The cannery informed me that the trap was not catching fish. Apparently there was a hold-up out where fish were escaping, or perhaps a playing whale or shark had punched a ten-foot hole through the wire.

While I was still a hundred yards from the trap, a boat pulled away. It was the same black-hulled boat the three young fishermen had been working on. The men waved as we passed. The big fellow with the whiskers called, "How goes it, Diver?"

"Fine," I shouted. "How is it with you?"

"Couldn't be better." He made an O with thumb and finger.

I dived the trap and found nothing wrong. Afterward, sitting in the shack drinking coffee, I asked the watchman, "Those three fellows in the boat, friends of yours?"

He looked at me over the coffee cup. "Why?" he asked in a careful voice.

I told him of the happening on the cannery dock and the superintendent's threats. "I thought you might meet me with a rifle," I said.

"Bunk! No watchman is going to dodge bullets for a cannery for three-hundred-fourteen dollars a month. That was bluff. The super knew it and so did those boys. The cannery makes those threats every season but nothing ever happens."

I didn't answer, and he ran on as though he expected me to know all about it. "I figured you was wise the minute you saw them tied to the trap. Well, they made me a good deal, so I took it. They pay me a dime a fish for all I let them take out of the trap. I figure to go outside this fall with an extra four thousand bucks. It's money right on the barrelhead. No arguments." He finished his coffee, then asked abruptly, "How come you're diving the trap? I didn't send for you."

"The cannery said it wasn't fishing."

"Hm-m-m," he said, "it's fishing all right. They're getting the fish, too. But they don't know that—or do they? Maybe I had better ease up a little, before they get too suspicious."

"Suppose you had said no when they propositioned you?"
I asked.

"It wouldn't have made any difference to them. Plenty of
other trap watchmen are anxious to work for them."

The time I dove the trap at Eagle Point, a storm boomed
out of the Aleutians and caught me. I ran into Andersen Bay
to lay it out. I was tying up to a dolphin, when another
boat nosed up beside me. She was around fifty feet, and
painted a camouflage battleship gray. The color was the first
giveaway. Practically all pirate boats are painted a dark, water-
blending color, making them hard to spot from the air or
from a distance at sea. The name on her bow was that of one
of the most famous pirate boats in the North.

The stories I had heard of this nervy skipper and his boat
were legion. This fellow even had a trap brail, a special sort
of dip net for taking fish from a trap. It is supposed to be used
only by the cannery tenders whose job is to empty the trap.
Unlike the round, sock-shaped brail used by the seiners, the
trap brail is flat as a blanket, and is some twenty feet wide by
forty feet long. This brail was fastened to his boom in plain
sight—a billboard advertising his trade.

The temptation was too great. After I had finished tying
up, I jumped aboard his boat. He opened the galley door
and called cheerfully, "Come in, man, before you blow overboard."

I introduced myself and he smiled. "I know, the diver. I
don't envy you your job."

He was middle-aged, tall, slender, but looked rawhide
tough. His hair was dark and his eyes were deep-sea blue.
His voice was quiet, his manner had just the proper degree of

friendliness for a host. He had the calm, efficient air of a successful business man.

We sat on either side of the table in his spotless galley. He got out and packed an old pipe while I found the remnants of a cigar. Soon tobacco smoke eddied pleasantly through the galley, mingling with the mouth-watering aroma of a pot of steaming coffee on the galley stove.

A woman came in from the cabin. She was young, nice looking and wore a beautiful tan. She scarcely glanced at me, did not speak to either of us, and the pirate did not introduce her. She set out cups, poured us coffee, then retired to the cabin and closed the door.

The coffee was good and the warmth of the galley and the smell of tobacco was like a drug, relaxing every muscle. We drank and smoked and talked fishing. I asked, "You getting any fish?" and immediately could have bit my tongue off, although this was a normal question you always put to a seiner.

He smiled. "I'm getting a few, but the run hasn't hit big yet." Then he said, "You get around more than anyone. Where are the fish running best now?"

"I saw a few jumpers off Miner's Point," I said. "But they're running good at Bligh Island."

I kept telling myself this quiet man was probably Alaska's most famous pirate but it would not jell. He belonged beside a fireplace, with carpet slippers nearby and a sleeping dog on the hearth rug.

He said, "I didn't hear of you until this season. You're new at this?"

"So new I let myself get caught in this storm," I said.

"There is no accounting for storms," he said. "I was born here and I got caught in it, too."

We talked about the size of the year's catch and the quality of the fish. Rather, he talked and I listened. He had made a study of the industry, both its past and its future prospects. The wind, tossed up by the shoulder of land behind which we lay, howled high overhead. Rain shotgunned the cabin windows with a steady, noisy drive. Night closed down black and tight. In this fish pirate's comfortable galley I smoked and drank coffee and was given a liberal education.

"The runs aren't what they were a few years ago," he said. "If I had owned this boat then, I'd have made plenty by now. There's no doubt the traps are doing us most of the harm, but then, we have more seiners in these waters than ever before—and we'll be getting more each year. In fact, the time is not far off when there will be nothing but seining whether the canneries like it or not."

"You think the traps are on the way out, too?" I asked.

"Without a doubt. But we will probably have them until Washington wakes up, if ever, and gives us statehood. By then I hope to have my own cannery." He talked enthusiastically about his own cannery while we finished the coffee and had our smokes out. Then I said goodnight and left.

Lying in my own bunk, listening to the storm slam by, I tried to associate the stories I had heard with this man. They simply would not fit. I wondered what had made him become a pirate. There was no reckless, daredevil air about this man, as there had been the three young fellows I had met. This man had intelligence, a fine personality, and he was a thinker. Such a man would have been a success outside in one of the big cities. What had kept him here, dodging the canneries' patrol planes and speedboats for the precarious existence of a fish pirate? Then I remembered a conversation I had had with Eric when I returned from my first swing around the Sound. He came aboard and asked how I had made out.

I was enthusiastic and happy, but a little afraid such a good thing just could not last. "I made out fine," I said. "I just hope I can get back again next year."

Eric misunderstood and said, "Oh, you'll come back. They always come back. I went outside for six weeks last year and couldn't wait to get back. This country—it gets into you and won't let you go."

That is how it must be with this pirate, I decided. He had been born here and the country was too big a part of him to leave. Here he was his own man, in spite of all hazards. And even the hazards, I suspicioned, were the spice of his life. No amount of success outside would equal that.

Next morning when I crawled out into a cold, soggy world the storm and my pirate friend were gone.

Several days later I went aboard a cannery tender with Oscar, the captain, and Swanie, the deck hand. I was to dive for a lost ten-ton anchor. I spent most of the day ninety feet down and found nothing. We were headed back for the cannery when the call came short wave to go and lie off the Bligh Island Trap overnight and to report all that went on. It seems that when the tender arrived to brail the trap the watchmen had been drunk and the trap was empty. For safety's sake, liquor is never allowed aboard a trap. The watchmen's only source had to be a passing boat, and liquor is often a pirates' chief persuader. It pointed to the watchmen's selling fish.

We pulled into position off Bidarka Point at dusk. Two

miles across darkening Tatitlek Narrows we could make out
the outline of the Bligh Island Trap. The land behind the trap
sloped gently into the sea. Any boat that approached would
be cut blackly against the night sky. Oscar grumbled, "I don't
like this playing stool pigeon. I've got nothing against those
pirates."

Swanie rubbed a suspiciously red nose. "Going to be cold
tonight. What we need is a couple of good big drinks." He
shivered as though already chilled. "We got time to go to the
trap and see if they got any."

"And give the whole show away?" Oscar demanded.

Swanie shrugged. "If they got a good bottle, who cares?"

I said, "If the pirates were here a couple of nights ago, it's
not likely they will come again so soon."

"That's for sure," Swanie said. "I start the motor, huh?"

Oscar scratched his jaw. "I guess what we don't see, we
can't tell," he said.

"Now you're talking," Swanie said. "I start the motor?"

Oscar would not let him start the motor, so Swanie did not
get his drink—and the pirates did not come. But if they had,
they could have taken every fish, built a fire on the trap high
as Mt. McKinley and fried them. We would not have seen
a thing. We slept like logs.

The cannery superintendent suspected what had happened.
The following evening he came out, and running quietly
without lights, slipped across the narrows into the trap. He
caught my big friend from Andersen Bay just pulling away.
The watchmen were frantically letting down the spiller again.
Fresh scales littered the headlog and the trap was almost
empty. As a final clincher both watchmen were half drunk.

The pirate went free. The watchmen were fired. They

frankly admitted, "Sure we were selling fish, but there's nothing you can do about it. Those fish were in your trap, but they were still swimming in the sea. They're not yours till you take possession of them in the hold of your boat."

That's what the pirates insist, too.

What has brought about such a seemingly lawful, yet unlawful, situation?

First: Alaska's fishing and pirating is somewhat similar to the prohibition and bootlegging era, when otherwise upright citizens registered their disapproval of an unpopular law by making their own brew. Second: and this hits the seiners where it hurts most—a seiner churns over hundreds of miles of sea, strains water for days barely making expenses, then comes on a trap with ten thousand fish boiling in the spiller. The trap, as always, is situated off a choice spot, where the salmon run heaviest and he could seine a good load. Now an eighteen-hundred-foot lead, hooked onto shore and running out to the huge log-frame trap, completely blocks him out. The trap is there year after year. It fishes day and night, and during storms when the seiner is lying behind a point waiting it out. Third: the Alaskans contend that the traps, due to their choice locations, catch all the fish and damage the runs— that traps are fish-killers, whereas the seiner is not. And the seiners complain that it is unfair to give the same choice locations to the canneries year after year, crowding everyone else out.

The canneries counter with the fact that the trap is the cheapest way of catching fish. Without the traps, they say, the price of salmon would be doubled to the consumer.

The Alaskans reply that salmon fishing is Alaska's main

78   *North to Danger*

industry, and that of the 438 traps licensed in 1948, 245 were owned and operated by eight absentee canning companies.

Absentee control of the fishing industry is so complete that Alaskans lack even full benefit of employment in their own major industry. The wages paid nonresidents are double that paid to residents. The bulk of these nonresidents come North from the States by boat, and they do not receive their pay until their return to Seattle at season's end. Thus, Alaska does not even receive their pin-money business. So, added to the profit in pirating, Alaskans feel a healthy satisfaction in striking a blow at the enemy who is milking them of their treasured possessions.

Fourth: and playing right into the pirate's eager hands— the Bureau of Fisheries has notified the canneries that the traps are on the way out because they are harmful to the industry. In fact, if for any reason a trap site is not used for a season, its further use is canceled by the Bureau. The primary interest of the Bureau's wardens in the pirate is when he tries to seine in the restricted spawning streams. This leaves the canneries to battle the trap pirate alone, with no law to back them up other than that against trespassing.

In an effort to discourage pirating, the canneries hire watchmen to guard the traps against pirates, then hire watchmen to watch the watchmen. They charter patrol planes and patrol boats to cruise the traps. Pinkerton men work under cover among crews, on traps, and on the boats. There are two-way radios aboard the traps, the tenders and at the cannery. Code is used in all reports concerning fish in the trap.

A cannery owner explained this cloak-and-dagger code: "If a watchman called and said there were fifty thousand fish in the trap, every seiner and pirate within a hundred miles would hear it. We would have seiners lined up three deep before the trap's lead, taking every fish that came by. At night the pirates would move in and clean out the trap." Some canneries use colors to designate numbers of fish in the trap. Others use units. Twenty thousand units may mean ten thousand fish. Forty thousand may mean only five thousand. Everything is done to confuse seiners, pirates and competitive canneries.

With all the money and effort put forth by the canneries to ensure against loss of fish, they overlook the one simple, sure method of stopping piracy. That is, by refusing to buy from the pirates.

Their own competitive greed defeats this end. A trip through a modern cannery makes that understandable. The season on pinks, the big run, is but a month long. During that time a cannery may have to put up thirty-five thousand cases before paying expenses. Profits are dependent upon an uninterrupted operation practically day and night. That means a continual stream of fish pouring into the cannery, regardless of where or how they are obtained.

As a cannery superintendent told me, "Maybe they are pirated, and from my own traps to boot. But if I turn them down, a competitor won't. And his cannery will keep running. A pirated fish in a can is as good as any."

The pirates use ingenious methods for counteracting the canneries' protective measures. They have their own radio code with co-operating watchmen. The watchman may come on the air at a given time and, sounding like a fox farmer or trapper ordering groceries through a friend, say, "If you're coming this way tonight, bring me a dozen loaves of bread." To a pirate lying miles away in a cove this means the coast is clear and the trap is full. If the trap is empty or the cannery tender is due the watchman may say, "I've got plenty of grub."

Of course, the pirate runs the risk the cannery has listened in and cracked his code. Then being caught can become embarrassing, but that is about all.

There is another signal that was in use long before radio. One towel on the line outside the shack as the pirate sails past in the distance may mean "no fish"; two towels, "plenty of fish, and the coast is clear." Others use lanterns.

Another class of pirates roam the sea as freebooters grabbing loads wherever they can. These boys will cruise close past a trap and glance into the spiller. Experienced eyes estimate the number of fish with uncanny accuracy. If the catch is good he will swing back, and as he passes will hold up a fistful of bills temptingly fluffed out like a head of lettuce. "Three, four hundred for the fish," he will call. If the watchmen are nervy and interested, they motion him in. Or the pirate may stop and argue prices, trying to strike a bargain.

I stumbled into such a situation one night when I had been called to inspect a trap. A whale had been playing about and the watchman, alone on the trap, was afraid he had nosed up and punched a hole through the wire. It was late afternoon when I arrived, and dusk when I finished the dive. The watchman and I were standing in the lee of the shack having a last word when we noticed two boats, minus lights, bearing down from opposite directions. Both nudged the trap, men jumped aboard and came toward us. Two held fistfuls of bills. "Five hundred for the fish in the trap," one said.

"I'll meet that. Here it is," the other said.

"Wait a minute! J-just a minute." The watchman was flabbergasted. "There ain't enough fish in the trap to sell to both you guys." He scratched his head. "Tell you what—flip a coin. I'll sell to the one that wins."

A coin spun. A voice said, "Heads!" The watchman nodded. "Your fish. Come on in the shack. The coffee's still hot."

We were drinking coffee when a crew member from one of the boats burst in. "Cannery tender's coming up from the point. We've got to get out of here!"

We rushed outside. The approaching tender was a black dot in the distance. The pirates piled aboard their boats and faded into the night.

Several minutes later the third boat nudged the trap and a man hopped aboard. "I was past today," he said. "I'll give you three hundred for the fish in the trap."

The watchman just stared openmouthed.

"How about it, three hundred?"

"Hell, no!" the watchman said then. "I been offered five."

"Man, there's not that many fish in the trap!"

"I say there is."

"No, you're wrong. But I will make it three-fifty."

"Forget it," the watchman said. "So long."

The pirate persisted. "Split the difference. Make it four."

The watchman shook his head. "Those guys that left just ahead of you offered five. They'll be back."

The pirate hesitated. "All right, five," he conceded. "But you're holding me up."

The watchman stuffed a fistful of bills into his pocket and we turned back into the shack, closed the door, and finished our coffee to the sounds of brailing.

6

I Become a Pirate

Several weeks after the coin-flipping pirate episode I was back in Cordova. The season was half gone and dives were becoming scarce. I dropped into a bar one night while killing time and found it deserted except for Vic Hanson and the bartender. This was typical during the middle of the week when everyone was on the fishing grounds. Hanson was unhappy. He had brought one of his crewmen in to the hospital with a broken arm. Now he was short a man for the remainder of the season. "It would happen, just when business gets good," he complained. "I've got to find a man for the rest of the season and I'll bet there's not one left in town." I knew what he meant by business; so did the bartender. Vic Hanson is a successful pirate and is proud of it. He is a big, blond, good-natured fellow who always wears a heavy plaid shirt and hip boots rolled beneath the knees.

Last season, the story went, a detective in a fast boat had vowed openly he would get Hanson. But Hanson had continued his raid on traps and had led the detective through some of the wildest chases and escapes the Sound had seen.

82

The contest became so hot it was talked about up and down the street and the detective had taken an unmerciful ribbing from fishermen and cannery workers.

Now the bartender said, "I can pass the word around that you need a man when everybody comes in for the week end. Somebody's always ready to jump to another boat."

Hanson nodded. "Go ahead. If I don't get a man I'm through for the season."

I moved down to the stool beside him and said, "How about taking me?"

"You're diving for the canneries," Hanson grunted.

"I haven't had a dive in almost a week and this late in the season the chances of getting another are pretty slim."

Hanson lifted his vodka, squinted through it at the light and set it down again. "This isn't exactly seining."

"Not interested in seining," I said. "It's too uncertain."

"How do I know you won't chicken out, if it gets a little rough?" he asked.

"I'm asking to go along," I pointed out. "But if I turn soft, it don't cost you a cent. What can you lose?"

"All right." He grinned at the bartender. "George," he said, "give my new crew member a drink." He tossed off his drink and rose. "Got to rustle up a lot of five-dollar bills for bait. I'll see you aboard."

As casually as that I became a member of a pirate crew.

When we were alone the bartender said, "You're lucky. I would have gone if I could have got anybody to take this job. You'll make money. Hanson made twenty thousand last season; blew most of it right over this bar."

I locked the diving suit in the cabin of *Number 9*, left her tied to the dock and went aboard Hanson's *Lady Lou*.

The *Lady Lou* was a forty-eight-footer and could carry eight or nine thousand fish. She was a typical seiner with a seine, turntable and a seiner's brail fastened to the mast. There the similarity ended. She was painted a dull battleship gray. There were two small hooks above her name from which a sack or board could be hung, blotting out her identification. The seine was for looks and in all probability was full of holes and had not touched the water all season.

The crew consisted of Vic Hanson, Swanie and myself. Swanie had quit the tender and Oscar to go pirating. "Can't make money on the tender," he explained. "And that Oscar was always yelling, 'Don't drink this, don't drink that, ain't good for the belly.' I been drinking this and that since I was a kid. I know what's good for my belly."

Hanson came aboard later with a case of whiskey and shoved it under the galley table. "More bait," he explained.

It was still light when we pulled out. Hanson planned on visiting a couple of nearby traps on the way up the coast. We had not been gone from the dock ten minutes when we noticed Eric Johnson's big tender keeping pace astern. Eric kept the same distance, about a half-mile astern, as we bored steadily up the coast. Finally Hanson said, "Eric's wise to where we're going and he figures to queer the deal."

When we came on the first trap an hour later Eric was still there astern. We passed within fifty feet of the trap and Hanson glanced into the spiller. The surface was pocked by splashes, and just beneath the surface I could see the silvery flash of salmon. "About four thousand," Hanson guessed. "We'd take them if Eric wasn't on our tail."

Eric was sticking in the same spot, about a half-mile astern, when we raised the second trap. This time we did not even pass close enough for a look. Hanson decided to pull into a bay and anchor for the night. "There's no sense going on," he explained. "We can't outrun Eric and we can't lose him. He can stay with us for the night but he's got to be back at the cannery in the morning. We'll just wait Mr. Eric out."

A little later we pulled into a bay, dropped the hook and rolled into our bunks. Eric's big tender followed and anchored a hundred yards off. "He'll go back and brail those two traps we passed just as soon as he's convinced we mean to stay here the night," Hanson predicted.

When we rolled out next morning Eric was gone. We began poking along the coast, contacting the traps I had dived earlier. It was late in the afternoon when we found a trap with some seven thousand salmon milling in the spiller. The watchmen were a grizzled old fellow and a young one with a head of wild black hair. They came from the shack to watch as we swung back and nosed up to the headlog.

Swanie tossed them a line and the young fellow took a turn about a cleat. We jumped to the headlog with Hanson carrying a full bottle. The watchmen gave me a startled look but warily said nothing. Hanson wrenched off the top of the bottle, saying, "A mighty dry day, boys." He handed it to the old fellow.

The old man drank, sighed gustily and wiped his mouth. "Didn't know how dry I was." He drank again long and hard, and passed the bottle to his partner. The bottle went around to all hands.

"A nice bunch of fish," Hanson commented, nodding towards the spiller. He held a roll of bills big as a baseball in one hand.

The old man nodded, his eyes darting from Hanson's face to the money.

"About seven thousand," Hanson said.

"Pretty close," the old man agreed.

Hanson extended the bottle again. "Long time between drinks out here."

"Too long." The old man took a long pull—and another.

The bottle made the circuit and returned to Hanson. He held out the roll. "Here's seven hundred. Your money, my fish?"

"Okay by me," the kid said instantly.

The old fellow scratched his jaw; plainly he was afraid, but he was tempted, too. Finally—"You fellows pretty fast?"

"Give us forty minutes. Nobody will ever know we were here."

The old man considered. "All right, make it about one o'clock. But you've got to be fast. Understand?"

"You can count on that." Hanson shoved the half-empty bottle in the old man's hands and we climbed back aboard. "See you about one," he called.

We pulled up the coast about five miles, went in behind a small island and nosed up close to an overhanging bank. We spent an hour getting the brail ready, checking the hold, the winch and tying sacks from the hooks on the bow to blot out her name. Then we were ready to rob a trap.

We turned in to sleep because we would be up all night. Swanie and Hanson were soon snoring. I was too keyed up to sleep and lay looking out the port watching the sun drop behind a white V of hills. Twilight spread across the sea. No breath of air stirred and no sound broke the stillness. A small breeze funneled through the open port, turning the compartment cool and heavy with the acrid odor of timbered slopes and the mustiness of tundra and sponge-soft meadows.

The hum of a plane poured suddenly across the water, thundered overhead and fled away into silence. The cannery's patrol plane was making its tour at dusk, hunting people like us.

Swanie and Hanson were up by eleven. I told them about the patrol plane and Hanson yawned. "Our snooping pal; I wouldn't know what to do without him."

Swanie nodded. "He don't see nothing, we know. The bank makes a shadow right over the boat at night."

We had a leisurely meal of bacon, eggs and coffee and at twelve pulled out for the trap.

The sky was midnight blue pricked by a single star shine. The sea lay black and mysterious and the *Lady Lou* seemed infinitely small moving through this immensity. The dense shape of the land followed on our right.

After a time Hanson doused the lights and cut the motor until it barely turned over. We drifted quietly forward. Far ahead, low on the water, a light shone through the night.

Beneath it the black outline of the trap slowly took shape.

Swanie went forward into the bow, picked up a coil of line and crouched, waiting. To me, we presented a sinister picture—Swanie, a black, intent shape, Hanson and I silently watching the approaching trap through the wheel-house window, the *Lady Lou* now a black-hulled, nameless boat drifting stealthily forward to nudge the headlog with the barest jar.

The shack door opened, the wild-haired kid came swiftly across the trap and caught the rope Swanie tossed. The old man moved across the logs and looked up at us owlishly shaking his head. He had probably finished the bottle alone, because he wore the beginning of a good drunk. "It's no use," he muttered. "I can't do it."

The young fellow said disgustedly, "Charley has lost his nerve."

"The plane was over early—real early," Charley said. "Circled us twice—right low. That means he's suspicious."

"We can be gone in forty minutes," Hanson called from the wheel-house window.

"The plane could come out clear from the cannery in that time. And this is a good flying night. No, it's no use."

"Okay," Hanson reached under the galley table for a bottle. "We might as well have a couple anyway." He jumped to the ogs and started for the shack. "Watch the boat, Virg," he called.

They all disappeared inside. I sat in the bow of the *Lady Lou* and wondered at this strange behavior.

Some twenty minutes went by, then the shack door opened and Hanson and the young watchman came swiftly across the logs. "Let's get at it," Hanson said. "Swanie and the bottle are taking care of Charley."

The three of us went to work on the spiller. It took but a few minutes to work the net up and the seven thousand salman turned the spiller to boiling froth.

I steered the brail into the spiller. Hanson handled the winch, hoisting the brail aboard bulging with fish. The watchman steered it over the hold. The only sounds were the *pad-pad* of the motor, the dry complaining of pulleys and lines, the thump of fish in the hold and the hiss of falling water.

Suddenly Charley's voice boomed out the open trap-shack door raised in drunken song:

"Oh, give me a home where the Finlanders roam,
  And the Swedes and the Norwegians play.
  Where never is heard an Irishman's word
  And the Polacks are jabbering all day."

The brail traveled swiftly from spiller to boat and back.
Swanie's voice joined Charley's: "Where never is heard an
Irishman's word . . ."

In a surprisingly short time we emptied the spiller. We
let it down, splashed water over the headlog to wash off the
scales. We were through.

Hanson handed the young watchman the wad of bills. He
went to the shack, and a moment later Swanie stumbled uncertainly across the logs to the boat.

We pulled away fast into the night as "Oh, give me a home
where the Finlanders roam" drifted across the quiet sea.

Swanie said thickly, "That old guy, that Charley. He can
sure bindle. Every time he tipped up the bottle it was just
like the tide going out."

We ran all night and the next morning sold the catch,
seventy-two hundred salmon, to the cannery who owned the
trap. As Swanie said righteously, "It wouldn't be hardly
right not to sell to them." The catch brought twenty-one-
hundred-sixty dollars. After the watchmen's seven hundred
was taken out, we split slightly more than fourteen hundred.
According to the split, the boat takes a share, and the rest of
us a share each. My cut for the night's work was three-hun-
dred-sixty dollars.

We took on gas, water and grub and were off again.

Two days later we came on a trap opposite a rocky point
where the tide was such a millrace that the watchmen stayed
in a shack on shore almost half a mile away. Swanie was

steering and Hanson climbed to the flying bridge where the
added height gave him a better look into the trap. We cruised
past, a hundred feet out, and even I could see the fish milling
in the spiller.

"A good ten thousand, boys!" Hanson called down.

"And we don't have to buy this load," Swanie chortled.
"We just take the whole works, hah!"

Again we hid in a cove, hung sacks over the hooks, obliter-
ating our name, and made the brail ready.

When the sun fell into the sea, fog banners rose off the land
and drifted across the water. A chill mist began falling.

"Just right," Hanson said happily. "By midnight it'll be too
thick for the plane to fly and the boys on shore won't be able
to see the trap. We can take our time and milk this one dry."

Again we came into the trap with all lights out, though
the fog was so thick we could have burned a thousand watts
and not been seen. Swanie handled the brail this time. I
steered the loads into the hold.

In about thirty minutes we had filled the hold; then we
began dumping flopping, squirming salmon on deck. We
filled the deck a foot deep, and when they threatened to
overflow the rail we stood the hatch covers on edge and piled
them higher. At thirty cents each it was a mouth-watering
pile.

Hanson finally called, "That's it, Swanie. We got a load."

"Just one more," Swanie begged.

We took "just one more"—and "just one more." Fish began slithering off the pile, over the rail back into the sea. Our
stern sank until it was almost awash.

"That's enough," Hanson called again.

"Just one more," Swanie begged. The brail rose, loaded,

swung inboard. Then came a rifle-sharp report, a cracking and snapping of ropes and the brail crashed down on the fish pile. The hooks holding it had broken.

We let the spiller down in a rush and got out fast.

The fog had become too thick to navigate and we crept into a cove to wait for daylight. Hanson switched on the radio to pick up cannery gossip and almost immediately the trap we had just robbed came in. They were reporting the robbery to the cannery. "We heard this racket out at the trap, so we rowed out to check. We couldn't see any fish in the spiller and there was scales all over the headlog, so we pulled it up. The spiller was damn near empty. In the bottom of the spiller we found a piece of broken brail. Somebody's lifted the trap."

"How many did they get?" the cannery asked.

"About ten thousand."

"Did you see any boats hanging around today?"

"Three or four went by. There was the *Sea Otter*, the *Pelican*, the *Snow Goose* and a big gray job, the *Lady* something."

"*Lady Lou?*" came back immediately.

"Yeah, I think so. *Lady Lou*."

"The *Sea Otter* and *Pelican* are here at the cannery now. . . ."

Another voice cut in. "This is the *Golden King*. I was in Cordova tonight and the *Snow Goose* is there on the grid with a hole in her bow."

A third voice said, "This is the *North Wind*. I saw the *Lady Lou* laying behind a point not more than two miles from the trap at sundown. I took a look through the glasses and they had hung something over her name. But I knew her all right."

Hanson snapped off the radio and said dryly, "I would say there is no doubt who the guilty party is."

"None at all," Swanie agreed sagely. "But how they going to prove it? Fish are fish. I tell you, what we need is a good big drink and some sleep." He dug out a bottle and we had a drink. Swanie and Hanson slept, too. But there was no sleep for me.

It was nearly noon when we pulled into the cannery from whose trap we had lifted the fish. Hanson had gone there because it was the nearest cannery and fish are highly perishable. The superintendent came down, looked at our load and said pointedly, "Hanson, that sure looks like a trap-caught load to me."

"No such thing. We seined these," Hanson insisted. "Do you want them or not?"

"It still looks trap caught to me," the superintendent insisted, "and it does to you, too." He noticed our brail was missing then and said, "I see you lost your brail."

"We broke it on a snag," Hanson said promptly.

"I can believe that," the superintendent said evenly. "If you'll go back to that trap where you stole these fish the boys will give you the broken piece they fished out of the spiller."

"I'm not going to stand here and argue with you," Hanson said. "If you're not interested in almost ten thousand fish, say so and we'll shove off."

"Oh, I'll take the load," the superintendent said angrily. "Just don't get the idea you're kidding anybody." With that he stalked back into the cannery.

If I still had any doubts as to the fish pirate's immunity from punishment, the humorous article in the Ketchikan *Daily News* of August 11, 1950, would have dispelled it:

It seems there is a movement on foot to organize a union of trap-watchmen to put a minimum price on salmon sold to pirates. A delegate appeared in a rowboat at a trap in the vicinity of Ketchikan last Thursday. He proposed that all watchmen agree to sell no fish for less than $200 a thousand. He explained that pirates will be numerous this year and the opportunities for watchmen to make easy money are much better than in the past.

The boys had better watch their step or they'll be hauled up for violation of the anti-trust act.

Captain Kidd and Jean Laffitte must be turning over in their graves.

7

Danger in a Fish Trap

I do not like to meet undersea life inside a fish trap. They are cornered and so am I. Of them all, the sea lions and sharks cause me the greatest worry. Both are small enough to stay inside a trap, yet big enough to finish me off if they desire.

The sea lions are always cruising about the outside of the trap hunting a way to get in. Once inside they go wild, dashing madly, ripping a bite from each fish but devouring none. In a matter of minutes one sea lion can kill several hundred fish.

The shark usually blunders into the trap after he hits the lead and follows it out. Then he will lie on the bottom of the heart and stampede the timid salmon back out of the trap while he enjoys a Roman banquet.

In Alaska it is usually the basking shark I have to deal with. He is the world's second-largest shark, some going almost thirty feet, and so called because he loves to lie on the surface and bask in the sun. The book says he is harmless, but several things lead me to believe otherwise. Those long rows of band-

94

saw teeth are anything but reassuring and any fish twice the length of a man, with the known strength, speed and tremendous appetite of a shark, is no trout.

My first experience with the shark came when I went down for an inspection dive before the season opened. The wire had been down about a week. The salmon run had not started and the trap was empty. At least I thought it was—until I hit bottom about fifty feet down inside the heart and stared into the ugly faces of four big sharks which materialized out of the gloom. They stopped about ten feet off and looked me over. They were thin and hungry looking. I guessed they had been trapped here since the wire went down.

I stood my sea bottom and glared back at them. "They just look tough," I told myself. "The basking shark will not attack a man—if these are basking sharks." Then they came slowly toward me, all business. I was close to the side of the trap so I lifted the wire, ducked under and dropped it. All four lined up, snouts to the wire, and stared through at me.

They were not more than six feet off and I was afraid to back off farther. My air line came down inside the trap past their snouts and any movement on my part would move the air line and might draw their attention to it. After a little they became disgusted and swam away. I scooted back into the trap, hung the wire on a knot, hoping they would find the hole later, and shot to the surface. When I returned to bottom the next morning they were gone.

Removing a shark from a trap presents a problem. Sometimes he will surface and the watchman can get a crack at him with a rifle. On rare occasions a watchman may hook one, as happened at the Freemantle Point Trap. The watchman saw the shark just under the surface and stabbed down at him

with a pike pole. He missed with the point but snagged the
shark under the chin with the four-inch barb. Clinging to the
pole with both hands he toe-danced the length of the slippery
logs and led the docile shark back out to sea and turned him
loose. Usually they lower the Sunday apron and attempt to
drive him out. The Sunday apron is a section of wire, resem-
bling a gate, that is opened to let the salmon escape back to sea
over the week end, when the law says no fish must be caught.
When all else fails the call goes out—"There is a shark in the
trap. Send the diver to take him out."

The first time I had to go down after a shark I was at a loss
what to do. The cannery boat was standing by when I arrived. Both watchmen said they had glimpsed the shark several times but he refused to surface.

The skipper, a grizzled veteran, saw I was stumped and said,
"You take the three-eighths towing cable from the winch,
make a lasso out of it and go down and drop it over his tail.
Soon as you do that come up close to the wire where you'll
be out of the way. Soon as your helmet breaks the surface
we'll go to work on him with the winch."

The tender put the helmet on and locked it. I picked up the
cable, stood fiddling with the air adjustment and looking at
the trap. It was about eighty feet across the heart, and sixty
feet deep. Somewhere in those sixty feet lurked a submarine
monster. I could, conceivably, sink down right into his waiting jaws, or as I had heard once happened to another diver,
straddle him. The story went, the shark had charged to the
surface like a bucking bronco, the diver still stuck to his back.
It had hit the trap wire full speed, ripped through, and wiped
the diver off as it escaped.

"Well," I thought, "if you've got to ride a shark or get a leg bit off, this is as good a time as any," and leaped into the sea.

I went straight to bottom and stood looking around. It was fairly clear and I saw a number of salmon. But no shark. I moved toward the center of the heart, had gone about a third of the way across when I saw him. He was a little ahead and about ten feet above me. He looked to be about twelve feet long. He floated there completely still and I could see all too plainly his ugly, elongated snout and cruel, traplike mouth. He looked sleek and trim and deadly.

I stood there a minute letting my heart settle back to its proper place. Then I moved cautiously to a position aft of his tail, took a careful look at his head to see if he was watching me, inflated the suit with minutest care and floated up slowly beneath him. At the last second I dropped the loop gingerly over his tail. At the same instant I hit the chin valve, plummeted back to bottom, scuttled to the edge of the trap and shot to the surface.

The moment the helmet broke water, the winch aboard the boat rattled, the cable came taut. The inside of the trap exploded in boiling geysers of water and yards of foam. The shark lunged straight across the trap to the end of the cable and hung there, straining mightily. The boat listed, the winch rattled, the cable continued to wind in steadily with the shark fighting every inch of the way.

Slowly the shark was drawn across the heart, hoisted half out of water and held squirming and threshing while a man with a high-powered rifle emptied the magazine into his spine, killing him.

I took it for granted this underwater rodeo act would always come off the same way. I would always slip the noose over the shark's tail. He would always lie peacefully still, always pull straight away. I had a rude awakening coming. I got it at the Cedar Bay Trap.

There was a big fellow in the trap, the watchman said. I got into the suit, took the towing cable, stepped off into the heart and went to bottom.

I had taken about three steps when I was under him and so close I could almost reach up and scratch his belly. If I had jumped a little farther out I would have landed astride him. He was as big as the first one I had lassoed, and the way he lay there, like a log, completely indifferent to me, I was sure he was nice and logy and full of fish. I floated up aft of his tail and carelessly tossed the loop over it. The instant the cable touched him he exploded into violent action. The sudden lash of his tail barely missed me as I plummeted back to bottom. He lunged across the heart before the winch could take up the slack. Then he circled, beating the water to a froth.

I crouched against the side of the trap, praying he would not hit the air line. If he did, he would rip it loose from the helmet like so much thread and that would be the end of me. I grabbed the line, pressed it against the wire and waited.

Twice that big fellow circled the heart and it seemed to me he got madder and faster each time. Then the winch took hold. He lunged straight away to the far side and hung there, straining against the steady pull. I went up the wire like a scared cat. The only sharks I take for granted now have a spineful of rifle slugs.

I have never taken a live sea lion from a trap. The watchmen can always eliminate him with a rifle. He sits on the edge of the trap and fires at the sea lion's head each time he surfaces to breathe. Eventually he will score a kill.

In spite of the watchmen's sure kills, sea lions have caused me some anxious moments.

They appear with startling suddenness and their dispositions are unpredictable. A sea lion may be as much as thirteen feet long and weigh up to three quarters of a ton. His speed under water is such that he can run down and capture a salmon. Once roused he is a savage fighter.

At one trap a thousand-pounder got into the spiller and the watchmen had no rifle. When the tender tried to brail the trap, the sea lion crashed about in the brail, threatening to wreck it. A fisherman rowed out in the skiff and whacked him over the back to drive him off. The sea lion threw both flippers over the stern of the boat, heaved himself aboard and flopped after the man, teeth gnashing. The fisherman dove into the water and swam for the edge of the trap. The sea lion held the crew at bay until a boat arrived with a gun.

I have seen a sea lion, which had been shot, charge the boat and keep coming until he sank.

Remaining motionless is usually the best thing a diver can do when a sea lion appears unexpectedly. It is probably what saved me one day when I was right in the middle of patching a hole in the wire. He was a little fellow, a baby, about six feet long, weighing around three hundred pounds, and he appeared out of nowhere and slammed right against the face plate almost bowling me over. His mouth was plastered against the glass as though kissing it, and there I was, my face just the thickness of the glass away.

My first thought, as usual, was the air line. The old saw about a man's life hanging by a thread is literally true with the diver. The thread is his air line. I held perfectly still for as long and passionate a kiss as I ever hope to experience. I

looked at his teeth. I looked down his throat—and began to
sweat. I thought of slapping him and driving him off. But
maybe, in his present mood, he would take that for play and
snap at the air line. I thought of pulling back, wiggling the
helmet and breaking the contact. I thought of a lot of things
and discarded each one because my air line was but a foot
above his mouth. There was only one thing to do—sweat it
out.

After what seemed a long time he suddenly backed off,
made a fast circle around me and slapped against the face plate
again. Once more I looked at his teeth, his throat, his whiskers,
his eyes. He held the kiss a long time, then backed off again,
circled me and returned. I braced for the shock of his mouth
hitting the glass; but he stopped a foot short and hung there
staring at me.

He was making to kiss me again when I had a thought. I
lifted my arm, hauled back the rubber cuff and shot a solid
stream of air bubbles into his face. He disappeared in a blurr
of speed.

I have met but one sea lion who refused to be frightened by
a stream of bubbles. That fellow was a brute of an animal
who hung out in a nest of rocks about half a mile from one of
the traps.

The first time I saw him he was sitting on a rock about ten
feet high, surrounded by his harem. From two hundred yards
off I cut the motor, let the boat drift and looked at him
through the rifle's telescopic sight. He was an old fellow, the
biggest I had ever seen. He would go twelve or thirteen feet
and weigh close to three quarters of a ton.

I put the cross hairs on the smooth bulge of his great neck
and caressed the trigger. I could kill him and save a lot of fish

for the cannery. In one season such a giant would eat hundreds, maybe thousands. But I was no cannery owner, fisherman or trap watchman. I was a diver and the big fellow was not bothering me. The way he sat there, proud, unafraid, with his harem about him, the sea crashing beneath him, and the rugged land rising at his back, he was a symbol of the Alaska I loved. I shifted the muzzle an inch and drove a shot at the rock beside him. He sailed off the rock into the sea with a mighty splash, followed by his harem.

I saw him often those early preseason days. He was in my direct line of travel as I ran back and forth inspecting traps. Trying to surprise him became a game between us. As I came within sight of the rock I would cut the motor and try to drift in close enough to scare him into the sea with a shot. But his ears were sensitive and his eyes keen. I was more apt to find him swimming alone near the rocks, head turned, watching me with smug satisfaction.

If he was not immediately in sight, he might pop up suddenly within a few feet of the drifting boat, then give me a gravely curious old-man stare. He knew the sea was his protection. The moment I made a motion to swing the gun toward him, his head magically disappeared. There was no knowing where he might surface next, give a brief, derisive flip of his broad tail and dive again.

The two young watchmen aboard the nearby trap had seen him, too. Nick, the oldest, said, "He's been hanging around here lately. That big lug knows what a trap is for. He's gun smart, too. Always keeps you guessing where he's going to surface next. All we ever get at him is snap shots. Soon as the run starts, and we get fish in the trap, we're going to have trouble with him."

On one run between traps, night caught me as I was passing the big fellow's rocks. I lay that night in the sheltered little cove between the rocks and shore. I was sitting on deck enjoying the evening when the sea lion's big head materialized out of the dark water, not twenty feet off. Keeping my voice soft as possible I said, "Ho, Big Fellow! Can't you sleep either?"

For a little nothing happened while he studied me with great round eyes, then his head sank without a ripple. A minute later he reappeared on the opposite side of the boat, staring at me. "I've got no fish for you," I said. "Go catch your own. That's what I have to do. Or go hunt a seiner if you want a handout." His head stayed there, his eyes continued to study me. "Maybe you've just come to visit," I said. "I'm glad to see you this close up. It's time we got acquainted."

His head disappeared again. It reappeared at the bow, then at the stern. Finally he moved leisurely off toward his rocks and harem, not bothering to dive or watch me. We both knew he was safe.

A few days later I heard that a boat had seined a load near the big seal's rocks. He had charged across the sea right into the net after salmon. They beat him off with clubs to stop him from ruining a thousand dollars worth of seine.

I did not pass that way again for several weeks. Then a whale punched a hole in the heart of the trap and I was called to repair it.

As I came in to the trap I saw the big sea lion swimming leisurely towards the lead, a hundred yards away.

I got into the suit and went down into the heart. The watchmen lowered panels of chicken wire to me and I fastened them over a ten-foot hole with hog rings.

I had just finished the job and was ready to come up when something smashed into me from behind. It sent me sprawling on bottom. I got untangled from the air line and straightened up. There was the big sea lion, not five feet away, staring at me. He looked enormous.

Suddenly he began circling me at full speed. I stood perfectly still, thinking, "If he hits the air line he'll tear it loose sure." On the third pass he stopped and hung before me again.

I thought of the little fellow who had kissed me. I did not want to be kissed by this brute. I lifted my arm, hauled back the cuff and shot a stream of bubbles into his face. He snapped at them, not at all frightened. I tried again. He backed off a little, then moved forward once more to study me with big curious eyes. I loosened the knife in the scabbard. If he charged I would have to fight him. But no mere knife would stop this brute. I thought of rushing to the surface, but there was no telling what action that might evoke from him. I decided to wait him out. He would have to surface soon for air. When he did I would follow. He made another circle around me, then shot almost straight up toward the top.

I poured air into the suit and followed.

The first thing I saw was Sam, the youngest of the watchmen, right above me, a rifle in his hands. The moment my helmet came off he shouted, "We got that big lug this time. He followed the lead right in, chasing a bunch of salmon."

I sat on the deck of my boat and watched a scene common to Alaska trap fishing as it ran its tragic course. I had seen this dozens of times, and while I did not like it, I fully appreciated its necessity.

But this time it was different. This was the big fellow with whom I had played a game of hide-and-seek, with whom I had talked in a small bay in the dead of night.

He surfaced now in a burst of speed, snatched a breath with an almost human sound, and dived again. A bullet spanged the water inches from his head. The watchman waited. The big sea lion knew he was trapped, that danger lay on the surface. But he must breathe. He surfaced on the far side of the heart, drew another shot and disappeared. He did his best to confuse the watchman—dashed suddenly out of the depths at each corner, grabbed a breath, drew the inevitable shot and went down.

He didn't have the whole sea to fool the man in now. The very sea that for years had been his chief protection had betrayed him.

His time beneath the surface became shorter and shorter. I had a wild desire to dash up onto the catwalk, snatch the rifle from Sam's hands, lower the Sunday apron and let the big fellow escape back to sea. But I just sat there and waited for the finish. It came suddenly. It always does. The sea lion surfaced tiredly, right below the watchman.

He lay there against the wire gasping. Sam took his time and fired once. "Die, damn you," he shouted. "Go ahead and die!"

The big head dropped, the great sleek body went loose. I watched him sink down through the red-stained water.

8

The Greatest Bear on Earth

One of the first questions an old Alaskan will throw at a newcomer is, "You killed a brown bear yet? No? Then you ain't a sourdough, Bud." He will usually neglect to warn you that when in Brownie's vicinity, it is well to have finger to trigger of the biggest gun you can buy, one eye on the bear, and the other on a tree to climb or someplace to run.

My initial experience proved you are apt to find the brown bear anywhere and at any time.

Winter was still in full swing that day Norvin Greek and I decided to go hunting. I had come North early that season bringing Norvin along to act as a tender. I had planned on some early dives around Cordova and Valdez harbors, but the bad weather had kept all work at a standstill. We found ourselves with nothing to do but sit and wait for spring. To break the dead monotony we went hunting. We hoped to raise a wolf, or at least a rabbit, for excitement.

From early morning until noon, bent almost double against the cutting wind, we swung over the frozen earth in our borrowed snowshoes. We did not find even a rabbit track. At noon, thoroughly disgusted and ready to turn back, we stopped in a grove of scrub spruce. We built a fire against a stump to get warm while eating lunch.

Norvin was opening the sandwiches beside the fire. I was twenty feet off ripping dead limbs from a tree, when there was a terrific snort followed by a blood-curdling yell. I whirled and saw the snow beside the stump exploding outward. Through this white boil was charging the huge brown shape of a bear, snorting, coughing and blowing smoke. Norvin's snowshoes were pointing at the sky as he turned a wild somersault to get out of the bear's way.

I tried frantically to run out of my snowshoes and crashed full length on my back. I lay there terrified. The bear charged down on me—and over me, kicking snow in my face. He lunged off across the clearing plowing a path like a bulldozer.

I scrambled up looking for Norvin. He was six feet up a scrub spruce, still climbing. That was the only time I have ever known a man wearing snowshoes to climb a tree.

I remembered, then. There had been a small hole in the snow behind the stump. That had been the opening to Brownie's winter quarters. The fire had acted as a false spring causing him to come rushing out to make up lost time.

The Alaskan brown bear is the world's largest carnivorous land animal, and one of the most dangerous. His appearance conjures up the wildest pictures of great cave bears strayed down from some prehistoric age. Some naturalists have said that these giant animals are the last living descendants of those huge prehistoric mammals which roamed this Northern wilderness thousands of years ago.

The brown bear walks the beaches and sponge-soft meadows with commanding dignity. His bearing is kingly, unafraid, as befits the greatest bear on earth. Bears are so common in America that we say "strong as a bear," "big as a bear," to emphasize the acme in strength and size. We are probably thinking of the small black fellows, or at most, the Rocky Mountain grizzly. The blacks would be as babies in a Brownie's family. The grizzly would be only a small boy.

For illustration—the record black bear in captivity weighs six hundred eight pounds. A grizzly averages about eight hundred. A fifteen-hundred-pound Brownie is no record and thousand-pounders are average.

A brown bear was shot on Hinchinbrook Island and hoisted aboard a tender. The boys wondered how much water he would hold. They shoved a hose in his mouth and pumped him full. Water and all, he weighed twenty-four hundred pounds.

Dr. Will H. Chase of Cordova shot a record bear that weighed twenty-two hundred pounds. The hide, unstretched, measured thirteen feet six inches long. His hind feet were twenty-one inches long by eleven wide and a six-foot man could not reach around his head.

Brown bear country is limited to Kodiak, Montague, Afognak and Hinchinbrook Islands, the Kenai Peninsula and a part of the Alaskan mainland bordering the Gulf of Alaska. Unlike most bear species, there is scant information on the big fellows.

At one time these great animals were as numerous on the Alaskan Peninsula as cattle on the Western plains. There are still evidences of trails three feet deep and four feet wide that have been packed to concrete hardness by these giants as they traveled through the lowlands and ravines. Bear trails have been found worn inches deep in solid rock where they had traveled for centuries.

About 1885 the brown bear's hide was in great demand among the royal family and aristocracy of Russia. From 1886 through 1889 they were intensively hunted and the huge hides drew fancy prices. But fortunately the demand dropped off in 1889 and the slaughter ceased.

The bear come down off the high peaks in July when the salmon migrate into the spawning streams. They hang out, almost in herds, in the meadows of waist-deep grass and brush patches where they feed on the coarse grass and skunk cabbage. They congregate along the streams where their huge feet have tramped the banks smooth and cut the meadows with deep, hard-packed paths. One of the most spectacular sights I know is that of a fifteen-hundred-pound bear plunging into a stream in an explosion of spray to emerge with a salmon wriggling in his jaws.

Overnight, it seemed, the air turned warm, the snow crept back from the beaches and meadows to the high hills. The pile drivers were out in force driving traps off designated points throughout the Sound. Tugs appeared, towing floaters to locations and anchoring them in preparation for the coming season.

I stopped at a trap site one afternoon to watch the drivers work. They were within thirty or forty feet of the shore's high bank and were sinking the last piling for the lead. The hammer was rising and falling with a steady *whoosh-stomp, whoosh-stomp*. The man on the top deck of the driver suddenly let out a yell and scrambled down from the tower. I glanced up. There, etched against the sky, was the huge shape of a bear standing on the edge of the bank looking down at us. Mad pandemonium broke loose on the working deck. The hammer crashed down on the piling with an explosion of steam and rattling of lines. Men ran, shouted, swore as they scrambled for guns.

It sounded like war when half a dozen rifles of various sizes and descriptions tore loose. Seconds later Brownie looked as if he had been run through a meat grinder.

The pile driver had been there for days, shattering the stillness for miles. All other forms of wildlife had disappeared from the vicinity long ago. Plain curiosity had brought the bear to the source of the racket. Had he possessed a sense of fear he would have high-tailed it away when the rush for guns began.

It is logical that fear, as we commonly see it expressed in wild animals, would be a stranger to the brown bear. His actions say plainly that he is big, tough, strong and knows it. He will not be bluffed unless he wants to be.

I experienced a good demonstration of this the day I went hunting with a 16 mm. camera.

I had stopped at one of the tenders which was lying in the Sound that noon. I had dinner with the boys, then made my preparations for the hunt. In lieu of a gun, I planned to carry two whiskey bottles filled with gasoline.

Bill Roberts sat watching me. Roberts had spent half a century in the North. His sixty-eight years sat lightly on a pair of wide shoulders and sturdy legs. His growling advice was blunt and worth listening to.

"What are the bottles for?" he wanted to know.

"Lugging a gun and trying to use a camera is too awkward," I explained. "I'll have these bottles in my pockets—that will leave my hands free. If a bear charges I'll pull one cork, pour the gas on the ground, light it and stand behind the flames. He won't come through."

Roberts scratched his wiry gray beard. "That's the dumbest thing I ever heard. Why, I've seen a Brownie take a whole magazine of .30-06 slugs and keep coming. And you think you can stop one with a couple of bottles. My God!"

"But all animals are afraid of fire," I pointed out.

"You're not talking about a Brownie now," Roberts said. "But go ahead. It's your funeral."

So I went.

In centuries past, the sea had gouged a bay deep into the brush and tundra mountains. The bay ends in a large round lake cupped by gently sloping sandy shores. The slopes are dotted with brush patches and tree clumps as though artistically planted by a landscape gardener. Beyond the slopes the mountains rise steeply into the sky. This huge bowl is known as Garden Cove.

I anchored well out and rowed ashore with the skiff. The usual flocks of sea gulls took off with crying complaints. An eagle screamed angrily from a dead snag, then sprang into the air and circled upward. I secured the skiff to shore with fifty feet of line tied to one of the diving shoes. That lead shoe would hold the skiff against any tide pull or wind.

For two hours I labored up and down ravines and slopes, camera ready. I saw plenty of bear signs—snipped-off skunk-cabbage blooms, torn-up grass clumps, and a maze of tracks—but no Brownies.

I was ready to turn back and was easing up a foot-wide bear trail when a bear stepped into it ahead of me and started down. He was a cub, about a two-hundred-pounder—too small to waste film on but big enough to knock my head off with one swipe. I stopped, sure that once he spotted me he would turn off.

He saw me, hesitated, then came on. Finally I took a bottle from my pocket, pulled the cork and spread a line of gas across the trail. I dropped a lighted match into it and stepped back feeling perfectly safe behind the two-foot wall of flames.

The fool bear came down to the fire and peeked around at me. Then he sat down in the trail and began to squall.

There was a half snort, half growl behind me. The cub's mother shot out of the brush and came charging up-trail.

I snatched the second bottle from my pocket, scattered the gas behind me and lit it. Now I stood between two walls of flames with a bear beyond each.

The flames did not stop the old female. She swung around them and lunged in after me. I leaped the opposite wall, practically ran down the little fellow and legged it up-trail. The cub stopped bawling and the mother immediately forgot me. She broke the one law I had banked on—that all wildlife fears fire.

When I returned to the tender I admitted to Roberts that the idea had not worked.

"The best thing to figure about a Brownie is that he'll do what you least expect," he said sagely.

Several days later I moved the diving outfit aboard the Watson brothers' tender, the *Pearl*. The cannery had lost a pair of trap anchors when a floating trap dragged in a storm. Anchors were selling at fifteen cents a pound in Alaska so a pair of five-ton hooks were worth spending some time and money searching for. We were cruising off Constantine Harbor when Harry Watson spotted a couple of Brownies halfway up an almost barren slope. Here was a chance for pictures out in the open. We anchored and rowed ashore in the skiff to look them over.

It was a gray, overcast day, on the thin edge of rain, not good for pictures. But bears, like gold, are where you find them. You take your pictures where and when you can, hoping they are good. A flock of sea parrots rode serenely near us; their orange duck-shaped bills and white banded heads were the only bright colors in a drab day. Near the shore ahead of us, a mother mallard herded half a dozen ducklings toward the mouth of a tiny creek. As we neared the beach a big Brownie sauntered from a patch of brush. The sea parrots rose off the water, sped several hundred yards farther out and splashed to rest again. The mallard and ducklings dived into the mouth of the stream to disappear.

The brown bear, a big fellow, padded ponderously to the water's edge and stood calmly looking toward us.

"He'll beat it when we get close enough," Harry said and kept rowing.

Brownie waited. At about a hundred feet he reared to his full imposing height and swung his black nose right and left, sampling the breeze.

Harry held the boat steady while I took pictures. Then we pulled up the beach, heading for a distant point to land. Brownie dropped back on all fours and padded along the water's edge following like a dog. When we made the point he was there waiting. Harry rested on the oars and we studied the situation. Brownie sat back on his haunches, sniffed the faint breeze, waiting too.

"That baby's an old bear and probably ugly as the devil,"

Harry finally said. "He's got no intention of letting us land. You had better take him."

I used the bow for a rest, drew a bead on his broad chest and fired. Brownie whirled and began to run, not away, but parallel with us. The second shot took him behind the huge brown shoulder and produced no more visible effect than the first. The third found the head and he folded up and plowed on his face in the beach sand.

We landed and Harry squatted beside him running his hand over the heavy fur, murmuring, "You big dope. You damn big dope. If you had any sense you'd stay off the beach."

There was no use following the other two. They were wandering far up the slope, not running away, just continuing on a course they had set for themselves. The sound of the gun had disturbed them in no way.

It was doubtful, we decided later, if the bear I had shot had really seen us. Their eyes are notoriously weak. On several occasions I have moved in on a bear in a meadow to see how close I could get. At an average of about a hundred feet the bear would snort and rear suddenly skyward to look me over. Then I would begin backing away. In another fifty or sixty feet he would begin swinging his big head right and left, casting for my scent on the breeze, listening for the *swish-swish* of my feet through the long grass.

Their ears are so sharp they have caught the soft whirring of a movie camera more than fifty feet away. This keen hearing makes a bear which has been stung by a rifle an especially tricky and ugly character. He may take off at the first whisper of trouble, or he may do as Ted Brown's bear did.

Tramping the beach one day to stretch his sea legs, watchman Ted Brown rounded a down tree and met a bear face to face. He fired twice with a .22 to scare him off. The shots were as effective as bee stings. The bear promptly charged. Ted raced for the nearest scrub spruce and scrambled into its low branches. The bear raged about the tree roaring, growling and ripping off slabs of bark to within a foot of Ted's legs. It was six hours until the bear's temper cooled and he wandered off and disappeared. Ted waited another half hour, then dropped to the ground and legged it for the beach.

Several days later I stopped by the trap to borrow bacon and bread and heard the story. "Tell you what," Ted finished, "I'll make you a proposition. Get rid of that bear for me and I'll throw in a couple of cans of pineapple and peaches and a first-class steak."

The thought of a bear treeing a man like a squirrel intrigued me, and I needed the grub. "It's a deal," I said.

In a three-hour hunt I found but one bear. I have every reason to believe it was the one which had treed Ted Brown.

I had hiked up the beach several miles and was on the way back. I made no effort to be quiet because I had passed this way once and found nothing. My careless feet apparently wakened the bear from a nap beside un uprooted stump. He reared suddenly out of the long grass looking straight at me. He was some fifty yards off, well beyond his range of good vision, and there was no wind. In all likelihood, if I had remained perfectly still, he would have forgotten his suspicions and ambled away. But he had so startled me that I automatically jerked up the rifle and snapped back the bolt. That dry sound touched him off. Instantly he was lunging through the grass at me.

I was once charged by a mad bull and raced him to a corral fence, and another time by a wounded elk that I calmly finished off. These were nothing compared to facing the brown bear. His ears were flat against his big head, his teeth bared in a savage snarl. All the hate in the world was in his face. Death was in his little pig eyes, in the gaping jaws. Death was in the crook of my finger on the trigger, in the steadiness of my aim. In those seconds I dropped back a thousand years. This was no sport. This was an elemental encounter in which I would kill or be killed.

I knew, too, that my first shot must strike a vital spot to stop him quickly. It must be between the eyes, a tricky, fast-moving target that must be centered on with the rifle, and struck in a fraction of time. Through the scope he loomed enormous as he bore down on me. Then the cross hairs found his head and I pressed the trigger. With the crash he folded up in a skidding dive. He did not move again. I looked at him lying there, twenty yards away, in the deep grass. He lay on his side, huge forepaws stretched toward me, the long, curved claws plainly visible. A ball of wind ruffled the fur at his shoulder. Behind me the incoming tide whispered on the sandy beach. Then the sweat poured out of me and I began to shake.

Keen as Brownie's ears are they take second place to his nose. He will rear to full height at sight or sound of man. But he will charge on scent alone. The hunter's only warning may be the heart-stopping sight bearing down like a tank.

I went ashore at every opportunity, to hunt and to see the country, to walk about among whatever game might be there.

One day on Montague Island I was crossing a grassy meadow when I heard the familiar half snort, half growl, and a bear lunged out of fringing brush at me. His head was down and he was running like a dog on a hot scent. I started to swing up the rifle, then I realized he was traveling at an angle and would pass me. I waited, finger to trigger. He galloped by some twenty yards out with never a glance my way. About a hundred yards past he stopped and looked straight out to sea. He had lost my scent in passing. For a little he searched the light breeze with his nose, then ambled off and began feeding on skunk-cabbage blooms. I tiptoed away.

The first shot at such a brute is all important. If it does not strike a vital spot he becomes more or less immune to shock and you have a fifteen-hundred- or two-thousand-pound kill-crazy bear on your hands. Four times out of five it will be in brush at distances from ten to fifty feet with all the odds favoring the bear. His supersensitive ears and nose will make him aware of you first. Your knowledge will come when he rears head and shoulders above the scrub brush to look you over. Dr. Chase killed his record twenty-two-hundred-pounder at ten feet. "I had been after him three years," the doctor said. "This day, suddenly there he was looking down on top of me. I just shoved the gun in his face and pulled the trigger." Such action calls for ice water in the veins, lightning-fast reflexes and a sharpshooter's eye behind the most powerful rifle you can buy. And sometimes that is not enough. More than one hunter has emptied a .30-06 into a charging Brownie, scored with every shot and yet paid the supreme price.

9

The Outlaw

It is not often one meets a rogue, or outlaw, brown bear. I met one on Hinchinbrook Island that I considered completely savage. Any bear is apt to charge a man. That does not mean he is a rogue. The rogue travels alone, has declared war on every living thing, including his own kind. The bear I met graphically illustrates how tough a Brownie can be and the chances a hunter takes when facing one.

The series of events that led up to the hunt began the day I was heading for Bidarka Point to inspect a trap. It was a bad day, with a strong, cold wind and squalls of icy rain. The sea was whitecapped and the deck of the pitching Western Fisheries *Number 9* ran foam from stem to stern. When I raised the Port Etches Trap smoke was whipping from the shack stovepipe. That meant hot coffee. I pulled in behind the protecting trap logs, tied up where the boat would not be stove in by the beating sea, and went aboard.

The watchmen, Matt and George, were lying in their bunks reading a couple of well-worn magazines. The stove was going full blast and the coffeepot was steaming on the back hole.

Matt, a short, stocky little fellow, was putting in his first season aboard a trap. He was fresh from five years in the Arabian
oil fields. Before that he had dived several years in the South
Seas. George was tall, dark, about thirty, already a veteran of
ten years aboard tenders and traps. These two frankly admitted they sold fish to the pirates—for a special reason. They
had formed a partnership. Their wages and fish-selling money
were to be pooled to buy their own boat with which they
planned to pirate next season.

George swung out of the top bunk and asked, "What'll you
have, Virg, warm beer or hot coffee?"

"Coffee, lots of it."

We sat and drank coffee and talked above the voice of the
storm. I brought them up to date on gossip around the Sound.
We talked about who was aboard what traps, where they had
been last season, what boats held the high catches, what traps
were doing well.

Finally I told them the story I had heard of the watchman
who had been annoyed by a big Brownie. The watchman had
borrowed a couple of sticks of dynamite from a nearby
miner and stuffed them with a foot-long fuse inside a salmon.
He rowed close to shore, where the bear waited, and tossed
the lit package under his nose. The bear grabbed up the tasty
dinner and started up the beach. Fifty feet later the dynamite
took over, and amidst a thunderous explosion Brownie shot off
in a thousand directions at once, cube steak size.

"That's what we need for our big outlaw," George said.

"What big outlaw?" I asked.

"The one that's been raising hell here all season. You ain't
heard of him?"

They told me a big bear had come down off the high peaks

the season before. He was a giant animal who patrolled the beach and meadows with a proprietary air. He carried a hate for man to match his size. Last season he had driven the watchmen off the beach each time they had gone ashore. One had finally borrowed a heavy rifle and went in to have it out. The watchman had met the bear on the beach at the edge of a brush patch. Rather, Brownie had found him. The watchman was first aware of the animal when he came tearing out of the brush. The man frantically emptied the rifle, scoring with but one shot. That one glanced along the bear's thick skull and ripped away part of his left ear.

Then the watchman dropped the empty gun and plunged into the sea, where the bear would not follow. He had clung to the trap lead until his partner rowed in and rescued him.

The bear had patrolled the beach all season, challenging them at every opportunity. Neither watchman had the courage to face him. They spent the whole time aboard the trap, praying a storm would not drive them ashore within the bear's reach.

This was George and Matt's first season aboard the trap and the big outlaw was back, patrolling the beach and meadows as before, daring them to come ashore, mad as ever that any mere man should question his supremacy.

"We can't even visit the shore shack without him showing up," George grumbled. The shore shack is an emergency shelter on the beach to which the watchmen can retire when the seas become too dangerous to stay aboard the trap. "This baby has been stung by a rifle. That's why he's so mean and clever at detecting anything connected with a man. I saw it once before in a bear that had been hit. But he wasn't as big as this one. This one will weigh a ton if he weighs a pound.

Whoever stops him will have to do some dead-center shooting with the biggest gun he can get. But it's got to be done.
We can't put up with this all season. Wouldn't you know it
would be my luck to get stuck out here with nothing but
a 22?"

I had a new 8 mm. rifle I had bought from a fisherman who
went broke in a poker game. I was anxious to try it. And I
had never seen a bear that weighed a ton. Wind slammed
against the shack. Through the window I could see whitecaps
marching toward the beach. This was no day to go hunting.
But today I had time. I might not get back again all season.
And someone was going to get that bear. The temptation was
too great.

I told them what I meant to do and George said, "I'd like
to go along but with a .22 I would only be in the way. Watch
your step, Virg. He's apt to be anyplace in a three-mile ra-
dius."

George took me in with the trap's skiff and I hiked off
across a rain-swept meadow. This meadow was a huge bowl,
surrounded on three sides by high, steep mountains. The
fourth side was almost level with the sea. The ground was
soft, laced with dozens of streams and dotted with dense
brush patches. I was soaked before I had traveled a quarter of
a mile.

Bear signs were plentiful. Skunk-cabbage blooms were
snipped off. Trails crossed and recrossed leading toward favorite fishing streams. In spots the grass had been grazed down
as if by a herd of cattle. I moved carefully, keeping in the
open as much as possible. Luckily most of the brush patches
were small and by circling them I could spot fresh trails going
in, and sometimes see through them. When it was necessary

to enter a large one, I edged in, gun ready. Every few feet I stopped to look all about and listen. A dozen times I thought I saw the broad back of a Brownie and started to swing up the gun, only to discover it was the butt of a log, a rock, stump or hummock grown over with a brownish moss.

I continued inland about a mile, swung in a wide arc and started back. I had seen no Brownies. Perhaps the storm had driven them temporarily to cover. That was where I meant to go. For an hour I had been pelted with liquid ice and frigid winds. I had splashed through a dozen glacial streams, some almost hip deep. I was soaked to the skin and chilled to the bone. The rifle felt like ice and was lead heavy in my numbed fingers. Record bear or not, my enthusiasm was well dampened.

Then I came on the big brush patch and saw the tracks leading in. They were large as small snowshoes, and were buried inches deep in the soft earth. The tough meadow grass had not yet sprung erect. I was but minutes behind.

I knelt and placed my hand, finger tip to heel, three times in the length of the back print. Truly this Brownie was a king of beasts.

The brush was thick. Shooting would be close and the bear would doubtless see me first. I would get one sure shot. Any others would be velvet. I had a moment of doubt. Half frozen as I was, I did not want to meet such an animal at close quarters in the brush, where there was no chance to maneuver.

Common sense said to skirt the brush patch and go on. But I had come looking for him. I carried a powerful rifle in which I had utmost confidence. And I might never get another chance at a Brownie that weighed a ton. Holding the rifle ready for instant action, with finger to trigger, I eased into the brush, following a bear trail twice as wide as a cow-path.

A fresh squall swept in from the sea snapping the brush tops and drenching me with freezing rain. The bear trail was soggy and slippery under foot. The driving rain and low, scudding clouds laid a gray, misty shadow across the land.

I stopped often to look and listen. Wind and rain drowned out any sounds he might have made and the thickness of the brush cut visibility to a few feet. I had progressed some two thirds of the way through when I came to a small grassy clearing. I was poised on the brushy fringe looking across it when the great shape of a brown bear lumbered over a far bank and rolled toward me through the misty rain like something out of another world.

The wind was wrong and he had not spotted me. I backed up, hit a stump and stopped with my shoulders pressed against it. This, I knew, was not the bear I was looking for. He was big, but he would weigh no ton. His ears, sticking straight up, were perfect.

I thumbed off the safety and waited, hoping he would turn off. He came straight across the clearing toward me. At about twenty-five yards I could wait no longer. I drew a bead on his broad, swinging head and fired. That instant he turned to snip off a skunk-cabbage bloom and the bullet tore into his shoulder. He jerked his head up and looked about. I worked the bolt frantically. His sharp ears caught that sound and he came plunging through the grass at me.

My muscles were stiff. My numbed fingers felt all thumbs. For the first time panic touched me. I was never sure where the next hurried shots struck. I am sure of the last two; they slammed into his shoulder at not more than a dozen yards. Then he was gone, crashing away like an elephant.

I leaned against the stump getting over the shakes and telling myself he had staggered off into the brush a few feet and died. In a minute I would go over there and find him. Only I would not. Half the hunters who have met disaster at a brown bear's teeth and claws, have done so because they followed a wounded bear into a thicket. One hunter I knew, was sure his bear had crawled off to die, so he followed—only to come suddenly on him in a thicket. Hours later his companions found what was left. If you are sure you have hit a Brownie hard, give the bullets time to kill or at least to make him deathly sick before you look.

A sound pulled my head up. For a moment I was sure I was seeing an apparition. A second Brownie was ambling into the clearing from almost the same spot. He stopped and reared to full height, trying with weak eyes to locate the cause of the disturbance. He was a veritable mountain of fur, rising head and shoulders above the brush. His head looked big as a barrel and his jaws wide as a shovel blade. His forepaws, hanging limply before his huge chest, were big as a man's hat. Though he stood almost a hundred feet distant he was so tremendous it seemed but a step. This was George's big outlaw. Even at a hundred feet I could see that part of his left ear had been ripped away. George's estimate of a ton had been conservative.

I began fumbling frantically for shells, then stopped. His sharp ears would pick up the clicks of loading. If he charged he would be on me before I could get off a shot. I was downwind from him and by the way he swung his head I knew he had not yet found me. I backed slowly, carefully, around the

stump, putting it between us. My feet did not even whisper
in the deep tundra moss. I backed out of the brush into a
meadow, my empty rifle in one hand, the shells in the other.

There I stopped, loaded the gun and thought it over. I had
a wounded Brownie in there. I was sure he would die. The
question was, when? I had another, the biggest I had ever
seen, an outlaw, suspicious and looking for trouble. That
brush patch was no place for a lone hunter, no matter how
good his gun. I could not spare the time to wait hours for one
to die and the other to quiet down. So I stole quietly away,
resigned to the fact that my hunt for the big Brownie was
ended for that year.

A few days later, at the far end of the Sound, I heard further news of the big outlaw from a tender captain. George
had gone in to the shore shack. The bear had met him on the
beach, and chased him to the shack, where George had
grabbed the ends of a pair of rafters, scrambled upward and
perched on the roof. Brownie had ranged around the shack,
discovered the door, broke it down and went in. For two
hours, while George sat helpless on the ridge, the big fellow
had wreaked havoc inside searching for food. "Somebody
will have to kill that bear before he runs George to death,"
the skipper laughed.

Then Matt and George reported they could see a hold-up
in the heart about twenty feet down at low water and I was
on the way back to the Port Etches Trap.

The job was a short one. The wire had balled up on a knot
on the piling. I hacked it off with an ax, the wire fell to bottom and I was through. The job had taken ten minutes. As I
was getting out of the suit I announced I was going to have
another try at the big outlaw bear.

"I'd go along this time, gun or no gun," George said bitterly. "But the tender's due. You watch your step, Virg," he warned again.

On shore I once more headed into the big rolling meadow. It was a warm, bright day, bad for hunting a vicious bear. In such weather he was apt to be sleeping in the shade of a bank or in the thick brush. This meant that once again I would be dealing with close, quick shooting.

I kept to the open meadows as much as possible and moved with extreme caution.

The Brownies were out in force today. I edged by three medium-sized ones feeding in the distance. A little later I topped a rise and looked down on a Brownie splashing up a creek, making the water fly. Another was calmly eating a salmon on the opposite bank. I waited until the wader had splashed from sight and the eater had finished his meal and ambled over the bank.

I hiked inland for an hour, saw two more, then turned back toward the beach. I had seen no sign of the big outlaw. Finally I came to the brush patch where I had met him before. There was the bear trail entering the brush, but the past week and countless other tracks had wiped out his prints. I eased forward, following the trail. I found nothing, not even the body of the first one I had emptied the rifle into.

A half hour later I came to the last brush patch separating me from the beach. It was a scraggly patch intermittently spotted with thick, junglelike growth and thin, almost barren spots. It was bisected by a wide, shallow creek.

I moved into it, still following every precaution. When I finally stopped to look and listen for what I considered the last time I was near the bank of the creek. An eagle planed out of the sky and landed on a dead snag up ahead. He sat a moment, then took off. A crow set up a noisy racket, then was silent. He started up again and flapped into sight overhead.

Suddenly his cawing took on meaning. I crept silently up the bank and peeked over into the creek below. A thin line of salmon were fighting their way across a shallow spot, half their backs exposed. Along either bank the grass was tramped flat and cut with huge tracks. It was an ideal spot for a Brownie to fish. But there was no Brownie.

I was still looking at it when I heard the sound to my right —a sound like brush scraping softly against a passing body.

I swung my head, saw brush move, glimpsed brown fur against the green of leaves. I caught the lumbering outline of a huge body. Then he stepped into the open heading for the creek. He was not more than fifty feet off and he looked bigger than ever. His great head, with its mutilated ear, was down as he sniffed along the ground hunting roots. Muscles bunched and crawled beneath the loose fur. His huge paws reached forward deliberately, as though with each step he dragged the earth back to him.

I was keyed up, and his unexpected appearance and nearness so startled me that I whirled and shot in a purely involuntary reaction. Even so, I knew where that bullet went —behind that massive shoulder into the heart.

He whirled with a growling roar and bit at the spot. Then in a single lunge he was into the brush and gone. I stood amazed. He had run!

I moved forward cautiously and peeked into the spot he had entered. There was no dead bear. But that shot had been good. He was going to be a mighty sick outlaw in a short time. I would wait.

I have no doubt that decision saved my life.

When I arrived back at the trap the cannery tender was there and they had just finished brailing. I told them what had happened and George was for returning immediately. "He'll be plenty sick by the time we get there," he said. "There is a guy on the tender has a brand new .30-06 I can borrow. Let's go."

With Matt along to see the fun, we started out.

George and I wore hip boots. Matt was in oxfords. Each time we came to a stream George ferried him across on his back while I carried both rifles. We had taken a short cut to the brush patch, so we approached from the opposite side of the stream. This meant crossing to reach the spot where the outlaw had entered the brush. For the third time I carried the rifles while George ferried Matt.

We had waded about halfway across, splashing along knee-deep when Matt began yelling, "Let me down! Let me down! For God's sake, let me down!" He was kicking and struggling and George had automatically clamped his arms tighter to hold him. I started to tell Matt to shut up, then I saw his eyes. They were sprung round, staring up the bank. I looked and my heart did a handspring. Lunging down the bank, every tooth shining, charged the outlaw Brownie.

I yelled, "George, catch!" and tossed his rifle.

Everything happened in split seconds then. From the corner of an eye I glimpsed George catching his gun on the fly, Matt falling backward into the water, both feet in the air. The bear hit the creek in an explosion of spray. My first shot took him somewhere in the shoulder. I worked the bolt with a speed I did not dream I possessed and George matched me shot for shot. The sound was an endless thundering roar.

The bear kept coming. He lunged through a wall of spray, seemingly untouched by the lead slamming into him.

Some cool corner of my mind said, "Two shots left. Then what?" I drove them into him. With the last shot that marvelous strength suddenly left him. His legs collapsed. He landed with a sodden splash that threw drops of water in my face, and lay still. My last shot and George's had taken him between the eyes.

We stood and looked at him. I was conscious of my heart settling back to normal again, of the sudden silence like a pressure against my ears. George automatically ejected the spent shell from his gun, but no fresh one rose into the barrel. He looked blankly at the empty chamber. It had been his last shot, too. Matt, dripping wet, was mumbling between us, "That was too close. Too close. Never again. Never!"

As nearly as we could tell on examination, every shot had taken effect. He would have died without the head shots, but not before taking at least one, and maybe all of us with him.

We tried to drag him ashore to skin him, but his weight was too great to move. We could not even roll him over. We finally left him there in the knee-deep creek, the swift water boiling around his big body as though it had been there forever.

10

The Siren of Cordova

Everyone in the Prince William Sound area knows Pete Nicholoff and his mail-freight boat, *Siren*. There are amazing stories of him and his exploits. At some time everyone on the Sound has seen the *Siren* churning across the sea, or nosing in toward some wooded beach where a cabin crouched amongst the willows. The *Siren* is always loaded with mail, freight, grub, medicine and sometimes passengers.

Twice a month Pete's five-hundred-mile swing around the Sound is the only connection with the outside world for some three hundred fox farmers, trappers, fishermen, miners and their families. There are times when the very lives of these people depend upon his deliveries.

Pete is a spry, stocky little man of Bulgarian descent. He is about sixty, has thinning gray hair, a friendly sea-browned face and bright eyes. His home in Cordova clings to the side of the mountain back of town, a block or so above the main street. Pete is married and has a son, Perry, and a daughter. Perry is a handsome, devil-may-care young fellow in his late

129

twenties. It is evident when talking with Pete that his family and the *Siren* are the prides of his life.

Cordova is primarily a fishing village, so like most of the other men in town, Pete took to the sea early. For years he seined or leased his boat as a cannery tender before he acquired the mail run in 1945. There is not a nook or cranny in the Sound that Pete does not know intimately—certainly not a family.

One afternoon the *Siren* nosed into Cordova's mooring basin and tied up behind me. This was the end of Pete's run. The decks were loaded with freight and bulging mail sacks. I went down to help unload.

"Virgil," he greeted, "you're not diving?"

"Diving has slacked off." The first rush of preseason inspection dives was over. Now it was a case of waiting for an emergency call.

"You should have been with us," Pete said. "We could have used you loading this stuff."

"I'll say we could." Sunshine, the always-smiling deck hand, popped on deck. "My arms feel ten feet long from all that carrying."

"Next time you need help, yell," I said. "If I'm not busy, I'll go around with you."

"We could use some help next trip," Pete said. "Those Montgomery-Ward catalogues are due about then. There'll be about a thousand of them."

"If I haven't got a dive," I said, "count me in." I wanted this trip. I would gladly miss a dive or two, if they were not emergencies.

So, four days later, I once again piled the diving suit in the cabin, locked the door and left the Western Fisheries boat,

Number 9, tied to the Cordova dock, and went aboard the *Siren*.

The *Siren* is a sixty-five-foot diesel job. She is painted snow white. Sunshine and Pete keep her that way. The boys like to say, "If Pete and Sunshine are in the bow, and a grain of dust falls on the stern, both are charging down on it before it can settle." The galley is spotless, the nine bunks neatly made up. You could eat off the deck or the top of the shining four-cylinder engine.

We pulled out late in the afternoon with a half-dozen bulging mail sacks; a five-gallon bottle of acid for a miner; boxes of grub and a package of medicine, doctor's directions, and a bassinet for the three-month-old baby of a radio operator at the CAA weather station on North Dutch Island.

That afternoon we left a mail sack at the cannery at Ellamar. We left the bottle of acid with a bearded miner who met us on the shore of a distant cove. At eleven that night we pulled in behind an island and anchored.

The three of us sat in the warm galley drinking coffee and Pete told me how he had come by the *Siren*.

Pete had lost his last boat, about the *Siren*'s size. He was looking for another, when the *Siren* came up for sale at a sheriff's auction in Valdez. The whole Sound knew the *Siren*. Pete made a rush trip to Valdez and looked her over. She was a mess—dirty, paint-chipped, badly in need of repairs. But he had seen the fine construction underneath and knew what elbow grease and loving care could do for her. The most he could raise was five thousand dollars. A few who knew his circumstances insisted he was crazy to even try. "Why," they said, "she'll bring twenty-five or thirty thousand and you

know it. Half the big cannery men and boat operators on
the Sound will be there to bid her in."

"I can bid until it gets to five thousand anyway," Pete insisted stubbornly.

"You can, if you make the first bid," he was told.

A couple of days before the sale luck stepped into the
picture. The story got around that a big man was coming
from Cordova. He had plenty of money and was bent on
getting the *Siren,* regardless of cost.

There was a lot of big-money men on deck the day of the
sale. Pete recognized a cannery owner from Kodiak and several others from up and down the coast. "Why, there was
more money represented there than I ever expect to see," he
said. "And I was standing right in the middle of it, me and my
five thousand dollars. Those boys could begin bidding where
I would have to quit. I was sick I can tell you."

Surprisingly, the bidding opened at two thousand. Trying
to play the big man from Cordova, Pete jumped it to three
thousand. Someone said three thousand one hundred and
Pete loudly said four thousand. He got some sharp looks that
indicated the big man from Cordova was identified. This was
the impression he had wanted to create. Someone said forty-
one hundred and Pete immediately said forty-five hundred.
A voice said forty-five-fifty. Pete bounced it to forty-eight
hundred.

There the bidding stopped. Little Pete Nicholoff with his
sweaty fists in his pockets, clutching his small roll of bills,
was suddenly the biggest man there. One of the happiest
moments of his life was when the auctioneer banged the
gavel for the last time and shouted, "Sold to the man from
Cordova for forty-eight hundred dollars."

"I guess everybody had decided there was no use bidding any higher when this fool would bounce it up four, five hundred or a thousand at a time. That was just what I had hoped they would think," he chuckled.

Now, for the first time, he owned a boat that could meet the government specifications for the much-coveted mail contract. When bids were opened again, Pete dropped his in. He has had it ever since.

"The government pays me fifteen hundred dollars a month for two trips around the Sound. The freight and passenger service are extra. Whatever I feel like charging, within reason."

"That's better than seining or working as a cannery tender," I said. "It's sure and year around."

"Sometimes it's better," he smiled. "Not always. I must have about six thousand dollars out for grub and carrying passengers I'll never collect. But what are you going to do," he defended. "You can't let these people starve or get sick. And they have to go to town once in a while to celebrate, even if I have to pay for it. It gets mighty lonesome out here."

The mail route has added fresh worries for Pete's family. It used to be that when seining, if the weather looked bad, he could wait. Now there is a limit to waiting, two or three days at most. So he often takes off right into the teeth of a storm.

"Every time I shove off in a blow, I can guess what my wife is thinking," Pete said. "She's remembering the time I was reported drowned at sea."

He had waited as long as he dared that time, but the reports gave no sign that the storm would let up. So one morning he put the *Siren*'s nose into and and began to shove.

It is a three-day trip in good weather. This time, the end of the fifth day found him still bucking the storm a long two days from home. He had picked up one passenger and a ton of mail and freight in Valdez.

It was early afternoon, but already getting dark. In winter you are through running by four o'clock. He was rounding a point to get behind an island where they could lay out the night in fairly calm water. In another ten minutes they would have been there. Then the *Siren* rose on a giant swell, rolled into a trough and came down with a solid jar, a splintering crash of breaking wood. They stopped dead in the water.

Pete dashed aft to appraise the damage, and discovered a needle-sharp rock had pierced the *Siren*'s bottom and stuck several feet into the hold like a driven spear. Water was gushing around the rock into the hold. He had been passing this spot for twenty-two years and had never known the rock was there. It took a minus tide, a giant sea, and a deep trough to drop the boat right down on top of it.

Most times when you hit a rock you are still floating. You have a chance to run for the beach or rig a patch. This time there was nothing. Pete knew what was going to happen. A big wave would slap the *Siren* broadside and roll her over. As she turned, her bottom would be ripped out. The end was as far away as the wave that rolled them over. Maybe five minutes. Maybe thirty. He had to get his passenger, the first-class mail, and his crewmen ashore. But in these seas the skiff would never carry them all, and the mail. One trip, going in, was all it would ever make. There was just one thing he could do. Maybe he could raise Cordova by short-wave radio and call out a float plane to take off the passenger and mail. A plane could reach them in less than thirty minutes. After that the crewmen and he could make out in the skiff.

He picked up Cordova immediately, explained the situation and ordered the plane. After that there was nothing to do but wait.

Pete waved a hand around the neat galley. "We waited right here, one scared passenger, the crew and me. I stood right there, at that port, and watched the seas roll in and slam against the *Siren*'s side. I never felt so helpless. This was my boat and I had waited a long time to get one like her. Every dime I had was right here; she was being pounded to pieces and there was nothing I could do about it. It's like watching your home burn down in your old age.

"With each sea I could feel the *Siren* shudder and grind on the rock. I found myself trying to gauge the size and strength of each wave. I'd tell myself, 'A little bigger than the last one.' 'Not quite so big this time.' 'We'll take this one.' 'Another big one!' 'Maybe this one is it!' I tell you I died a little. A ton of white water came aboard like a waterfall. Each sea was wearing that hole a little bigger, tearing and weakening the planking. It could not last much longer. I heard the motor still running and thought of shutting it off. But it didn't seem to matter. I let it run.

"The passenger said, 'It's been fifteen minutes. How long does that plane take?' He was getting more scared all the time.

"Ten minutes later the plane popped out of the storm clouds and swept low over us. I stepped outside, hung onto the rail to keep from being washed overboard, and began waving.

"The plane banked and came back, the pontoons almost slapping the whitecaps. It seemed about to settle on a wave crest, then the last minute jumped into the sky again. It circled and came in once more, low, only to zoom upward again. It began circling us at about a hundred feet. I could see the pilot looking down. He was making motions with his hands. Then I got it. The sea was too rough. A landing would wreck his plane. We would all have to crowd into the skiff with the mail and trust to luck—and we had to do it quick.

"Then it happened."

"I had been watching the plane and did not notice the sea bearing down on us. I did feel the deck move. It lifted and rolled. A wall of water spilled over the rail and almost swept me away.

"I didn't know then the pilot had switched on his short wave and was putting that scene on the air. Half Alaska and all of Prince William Sound could hear that broadcast. My family, in Cordova, learned of it a few minutes after it happened.

"The pilot was saying, 'She can't possibly live in these seas! What has held her together this long I don't know. It's just a matter of seconds. Here comes a big one now. This is it! Here she goes. She's rolling over! That's the last of Pete Nicholoff and the *Siren!*'

"I thought we were goners, too," Pete said. "The sea stood right over us. The *Siren* rolled so far the rail went under. The deck was awash. Then she swung back, righted herself. She began to rise. She rose right up until she rode the foaming crest of the sea. She was off the rock and still right side up— I'll never know why. The sea carried her a hundred feet and set her down in a trough.

"The engine was still running and I dived for the wheel-house. The engineer headed for the engine room. In no time we had pumps going. We fought that storm, and the sea outside the boat, and the sea pouring into the hold. We limped into Cordova hours later and we had taken everything the Sound could throw at us but we hadn't lost a postage stamp.

"When I walked through the door at home my family thought they were seeing a ghost. These Sound storms, I can tell you, are something to get caught in."

"Maybe you had better go back to seining," I suggested.

"I've thought of it," he admitted soberly. "But then, I get to thinking of some of these people. . . ." He shook his head. "I don't know how to say it. But when the *Siren* comes to them it's almost like God. You'll see tomorrow."

Next morning we were off early, skirting a rock-ribbed shore line as we plowed through a sea splashed with stream-ing sunlight. Our first stop was at a small float that jutted into the sea from a bushy bank. A weather-beaten one-win-dow house, made of up-and-down rough slab boards and narrow battens over the cracks, crouched on the bank. An old boat with *Rainbow* painted crudely on the stern was tied to shore. The thin little man who came nimbly along the nar-row float to meet us was whiskery and dirty. He wore an old blue stocking-leg cap, a brown Army sweater, several sizes too large, and grimy blue pants. He accepted a small handful of mail and asked in a plaintive voice, "You got any spuds, Pete? I ate the last spud yesterday morning. I fin-ished the last can of milk last night and I ain't had any bread in a week. I'm getting awful tired of fried fish."

"I've told you before, you have got to order more," Pete said sternly as he got out several loaves of bread, a pound of butter, a couple of cans of milk and a small sack of spuds. "One of these days something might happen to me and the *Siren*. You'd starve."

The man smiled, showing black stubs of teeth. "Oh, you'll get through all right." He gathered up the grub, murmuring, "I'll pay you sure next week, Pete."

We pulled back to sea. Pete explained, "He does a little fishing, a little trapping. He always means to pay. He'll give me a few skins this winter. That way I'll get part of it back."

An hour later we rode off a rock-jawed beach and watched a skiff, bearing a man, woman and baby, row out to us. This was Cliff Johnson and his wife, Betty. They were both young, under thirty. They looked clean and healthy and happy. The girl had bright black eyes and beautiful teeth. She held up the baby and said happily, "Look, Pete, he's gained three pounds."

Pete wiggled his fingers at the baby. "He sure looks better than he did two months ago."

"Was the baby sick?" I asked.

"He was dying; in fact we were all on the verge of starving," Betty said. "But the baby was the worst."

Cliff held the skiff against the *Siren*'s side while he and Pete discussed fishing and the outlook for the winter's trapping. Then they said good-by and left. Once again we were off across the sea.

I asked about that incident during the winter and Pete told me what had happened. There had been a storm and he had waited three days for it to pass. He had medicine and baby food for the Johnson's baby, and grub for the parents. Their larder had been dangerously low his previous trip. They and a number of others around the Sound, whose cupboards would be bare, sent him bucking into the storm.

Four days later, still fighting the storm, he rode beyond a line of rocks opposite Johnson's neat cabin. The bleak, wind-swept beach was deserted. No smoke issued from the cabin chimney. Pete could think of but one thing. He had seen death from starvation and it is not pretty.

Then the cabin door flew open and the man and woman ran to the water's edge. They began jumping and shouting and waving their arms. He figured with them looking that excited and happy, the baby must still be alive. But how would he get the medicine and grub in to them? They could not come out through those seas, and the *Siren* would be smashed to kindling if he tried to take her through the rocks.

Waves were washing over the bow to slam against the wheelhouse. Wind shoved the *Siren* over. A rain squall marched across the sea and dimmed the people on the beach. Pete knew what he had to do—hand-line a skiff ashore with a man at the oars to steer it between the rocks. The line would help hold it steady and they could draw it back against the storm. He had done it before, but never through such a rock pile. If the skiff crashed a rock or was sunk, the rower might drown. The rower had to be quick, strong and half seal. It had to be Perry, his son.

"Man does some powerful thinking at a time like that," Pete reflected. "I looked at those people being happy on the beach because I had come with food and medicine. I thought of their sick kid. I looked at the rocks, white water boiling

over them. Spray was exploding ten feet high. If the skiff
capsized, or hit a rock, Perry would not last a minute. For
a second I thought of trying to take the *Siren* in. But I knew
that just could not be done. Then I thought of pulling up the
coast to an island I knew. I could lay behind it until the storm
passed, then go back. But the storm might last another week
or two. And, according to the doctor in Cordova, the baby
needed the medicine four days ago. I knew the Johnsons must
be out of grub. The parents might scrape through another
week, but the kid never would. We had to get in there now,
somehow. I thought of hand-lining the skiff in, loaded with
grub and medicine, and not risking Perry. That was no good,
because I could see where the current would sweep it into
the rocks without someone to fight it clear with the oars."
Pete shook his head, squinting through the port at the bright,
calm sea. "I never did make a real decision, like coming right
out and saying, 'All right, let's go'. I couldn't have said the
words. We just loaded the skiff, I gave Perry the mail and
medicine and shoved him off. I've never been more scared than
I was those next few minutes.

"A sea caught the skiff and threw it straight at a rock.
We tried to hold it with the hand line, but couldn't. It cleared
the rock with inches to spare and a minute later skidded up
the beach at Johnson's feet. We almost lost Perry when we
tried to pull him back. A wave flipped the skiff over, burying
him beneath it. Johnson rushed waist-deep into the sea and
scooped him out before he drowned. When he was finally
back aboard Perry said the Johnsons hadn't a crumb in the
house to eat, even the baby food was gone."

Pete was silent a moment, then he added, "The kid looks
pretty good now, don't he?"

Our next stop came after a long run to Glacier Island. We edged into a small cove and anchored a hundred feet off shore. A weathered log cabin sat on the bank at the edge of the brush. Smoke curled into the sky from the tin chimney. There was no other sign of life.

We went ashore in the skiff with several letters, a half-dozen magazines and a book whose outer label read *Book of the Month*. We pulled the skiff onto the beach and climbed a brush-bordered trail to the house. Outside the door was a discouraged little ten-by-ten garden, in which struggled a few scraggly rows of lettuce, onions, carrots and a dozen scrawny strawberry plants.

A woman opened the door. She was plump, smiling and gray-haired, somewhere in her late sixties or early seventies. Her first words startled me because they were so different from what I had come to expect. "Pete, you have saved me from a slow death by boredom. I'm out of reading material."

"Figured you were," Pete said, "so I made a special trip." He introduced me and I immediately forgot her name.

She moved aside and we entered the house. We were in the living room. The floor was rough planks worn smooth and partly covered with braided rugs. There was an old round oak table and chairs, a couple of rockers, an old couch covered with a hand-knitted robe. Magazines were piled in stacks along the walls. Two sides of the room were lined from floor to ceiling with book shelves groaning under the weight of books. A youngster, about two, toddled in from the kitchen. In a corner, in a homemade crib, a baby lay kicking and gurgling happily.

The woman was putting cups on the table and pouring

coffee. She noticed me looking at the books and asked, "Do you read a lot, too?"

"In my business I haven't much time for reading," I said.

"I take time. Everyone should take time to read. I've read every book there. Many two and three times. There's nothing like good books. I'd shrivel up and die if they took reading away from me."

We sat at the table and drank coffee. Through the window I could see that trees and brush grew so close to the back wall that sunlight could never enter the room. I asked if she lived here alone.

"Just for a couple of months," she said. "While my husband and our son and his wife are fishing at Kodiak. These are our grandchildren."

The baby continued to gurgle. The little boy stood beside the crib, rocking it violently as he watched me with big eyes. I thought of this woman, no longer young, and these kids out here alone a hundred miles from the nearest town. If she fell, was seriously injured or became sick, she had no way to summon help. All three would starve to death. I voiced this fear and she smiled confidently. "Oh, Pete would take care of us. But there is really nothing to worry about. I've lived here forty-five years and nothing has happened."

She had come here the day after her wedding. She and her husband had lived in a tent on the beach while they built this house with their own hands. Their son had been born in this room some thirty years ago. She had never been farther away than Anchorage, Valdez or Cordova, slightly more than a hundred miles. She had not seen Cordova in five years or Anchorage in seven.

I told her Anchorage was now a city of almost thirty thousand. That it had paved streets, modern concrete buildings, hundreds of cars, parking meters and stop lights.

"Pete tells me that, too," she said wonderingly.

"You never get lonesome?"

"How can I, as long as Pete brings me good books and magazines?" she asked.

Outside again I looked around. "Almost half a century of gathering," I thought, "and what do they have to show for it? A tiny path from the sea. A ten-by-ten garden that would not even grow healthy weeds. A three-room log cabin without a single convenience squatting amongst trees and brush so thick that it remained perennially damp and musty. In a few years these people would be dead. The house, deserted, would rot quickly with this Northern dampness creeping through its timbers. The roof would cave in, the walls collapse. Soon the green jungle would grow over, claiming it again for its own. All signs that people had lived and planned and struggled here would be gone.

"Where's the percentage?" I asked Pete. "What have they accomplished?"

"Look at it this way. A man works at a job, jumps to a whistle, runs a machine or goes to an office all his life. When he dies, somebody else buys his house, paints it another color and remodels it to suit himself. It's another house with another family. Neither he nor the Alaskan has done much but live out his life as he saw it, and maybe raised a family. They both struggled and planned. The man up here has been his own boss and lived as he pleased. I think he came out on top."

There was no argument for such logic.

We churned the length of Knight Island Passage with the brilliant Northern sun swinging overhead and beginning the long fall toward the western snow peaks. A porpoise came out of nowhere, cut slashing strokes across the bow and disappeared. A flock of ducks skimmed the water, seeming too heavy to rise more than a couple of feet, or fly more than several hundred yards, before splashing heavily into the sea again. A whale blew up ahead and disappeared. A minute later he surfaced behind. The only sounds in the world were the creamy curl at the bow and the soft *chuff-chuff* of the exhaust echoing against the brush and rock slopes.

The sun had dropped half the blue arc when we finally rounded the point of Chenega Island and swung into the bay where the native village of Chenega huddled on a high, brushy bank.

Chenega is a dozen or so rough, weather-blackened shacks with corrugated iron roofs. Corrugated iron is common, because the deep snows will slide off readily. On shingles or composition it piles up until its weight breaks in the roof. Each house had one small square window, usually bare, facing the sea. The town looked deserted. The one splash of paint visible was the teacher's house. It sported a pink corrugated roof and white sides.

As we dropped anchor, doors banged open and a clamoring assortment of men, women and kids raced down the bank, piled into a conglomeration of boats and headed for the *Siren*. They had the appearance of a boarding party.

Aboard the *Siren*, all was ready. Pete had the mail out. There was a rifle for someone, a box marked FRAGILE, boxes of grub and a dozen packages of assorted sizes. In the galley the table held a mound of hard candy and two cases of pop from which the tops had been drawn.

The kids came first. They swarmed over the rail like a herd of playful otters, black eyes sparking, faces shining. They charged the galley, pushing and crowding to get in. I watched through a port as they swarmed around the galley table. I realized then, that here were the only sweets that many of these candy-starved kids ever knew.

On deck the older people were clustered about Pete as he handed out mail freight and boxes of groceries. A woman and man were wrestling the FRAGILE carton into a boat. A man was fondling the rifle, running a hand along the smooth barrel, smiling to himself. Amidst an excited babbling of voices, letters were being ripped open and read. Through all this a stream of questions were being fired at Pete.

An anxious mother asked, "You bring the medicine for my baby?" Her face dissolved in smiles when he handed it over.

"You see my brother? He all right?"

"He's fine, had the flu. He's fishing again, like you ought to be."

"How is the run the other end of the Sound?"

"You got any extra milk? I'm about out of milk."

"You got any extra bread? I'm out."

"They going to extend the season? You heard?"

A host of questions about relatives, friends. Someone had hit a rock and lost his boat. Did he get out? How was the bush pilot and two passengers who had flown into the side of the mountain near San Juan?

Finally the questions were all answered; mail, groceries and freight had been delivered. The two cases of pop and the pile of candy in the galley were gone. The kids were scrambling about on deck now, their cheeks bulging with the last of the sweets. People began moving toward the boats. The boats trickled back to shore by ones and twos. The rowers worked halfheartedly, as though reluctant to leave.

The *Siren*'s anchor rattled up. The big diesel throbbed softly. We made a tight swing in the bay and headed out to sea. I glanced back. A small knot of kids stood silently on the beach watching.

We cut across to Latouche Island and the ghost town of Latouche. A copper mine employing more than twelve hundred men had been in full operation here during the First World War. A fine dock, mine buildings and a cluster of neat homes had been erected. Ore ships beat their way north regularly to load the fabulously rich rock at the Latouche dock. Then about 1925 the vein played out. Now the neat homes were a jumble of shacks in various stages of decay half hidden in shoulder-high grass and weeds. The mine itself was a mass of twisted, rusting sheet iron, steel rails and broken buildings. There was the yawning mouth of a partially caved-in mine shaft with twisted rails disappearing inside. One building remained in passable repair. In it lived a man, his wife and two small girls. They kept a ghostly vigil over the dead town.

We left a package on the old dock and Pete added a half-dozen comic books.

We headed for Valdez, running down the long margin of Montague Island. The falling sun spread a golden sheen across the sea and touched the distant peaks with coral. Pete pointed to a bleak stretch of beach and said, "That's where Doc Allberry and Al Tibbett came."

I had heard sketchy accounts of that tragic incident which

still had all Alaska puzzled. Pete, I had been told, knew more than anyone. He had been called in on the rescue. I asked about it and he told me the story, as he knew it, while we bored through the fading day.

Dr. Allberry, about fifty, and Al Tibbett, a young fellow who had worked a season for Pete as a deck hand, went to Montague Island in the dead of winter. Some say they went to prospect for gold. But you do not prospect in Alaska in winter. Others believe they went to beachcomb. That part of the island faces the gulf and winter storms have blown valuable articles ashore.

"But," Pete insisted, "that doesn't happen often enough to make it pay."

One guess was as good as another. Everyone did know the two had hired a boat to take them to McLoud Harbor on Montague Island. A boat captain unloaded them on the beach with enough grub and equipment to last a month. At the end of that time he was to return for them.

The month passed. The captain said later that he had returned but found them gone, and no sign that they had been around recently. He assumed another boat had picked them off, so he left.

A second month passed.

A third month passed.

Still there was no word from the Doctor or Al Tibbett. The Moose Lodge in Nome finally took action. They hired Pete to look for the missing men.

Pete was reasonably sure no boat had taken them off the island, or someone would have heard from them. He guessed that they had hiked somewhere and for some reason had not returned to their original camp. He guessed, too, that they had probably crossed the island, from east to west, and had come out at Nellie Martin River. That was a logical spot to be taken off by a boat. Also, at Nellie Martin there was a pair of old trappers' cabins for shelter.

There were several big drawbacks to this reasoning. First, why should they walk across the island? And, assuming they had, it meant crossing three mountains almost three thousand feet high and tramping miles of snow-blanketed tundra in subzero weather. That hike would be an almost superhuman feat.

Nothing else about their trip had made sense, so he ignored the drawbacks and headed for Nellie Martin. Two days later Pete dropped anchor off the shore. It was a cold gray day with an icy wind. First dark was turning the snow lead-colored. The two cabins on the bank, surrounded by bare-limbed alders, looked deserted in the snow. There was no sound and no living thing moved. Pete looked out the wheel-house window at this scene, thinking what he might find in the cabins and dreading to go ashore.

Then, a couple of hundred yards up the beach he spotted movement against a bank. A figure moved slowly across the beach to the water's edge and came forward. For a moment he thought it was a shaggy old bear that had emerged from hibernation in the middle of winter. Then he saw it was a man bent almost double. The fellow stopped and looked toward the boat. He wiped a palm across his eyes, as though trying to clear them. Then he shaded his eyes with his hand and kept looking. Suddenly he began to run. He wobbled and stumbled like a baby learning to walk.

They put the skiff over and rowed ashore. The man met them on the beach before the first cabin.

"I had known Dr. Allberry as a husky man," Pete said. "Now he was small, bent, a skeleton lost in his ragged parka. His cheeks were dished in like mush bowls. The only thing about him that seemed alive were his eyes. He tried to smile. Then he whispered, 'I thought I was dreaming. I've seen a boat so often. . . .' He put out a shaking hand and pitched forward in a dead faint.

They found Al Tibbett in the second cabin frozen solid.

Back aboard the *Siren* the Doctor wanted pancakes to eat.

"Pancakes will kill you," Pete told him and poured a glass of tomato juice. "Get this down first. Something light."

The Doctor pushed the juice away. "For eighty-three days I have lived on a few mussels I found along the beach, and every day I stuffed my stomach with moss to keep it from shrinking. I've dreamed of pancakes every one of these days. I'm going to have them if they do kill me."

Pete fried him a pancake. He took two bites, vomited and fainted. They revived him and he tried again. He tried until the pancake was gone though he lost every bite. Then Pete brought out the tomato juice again. He set it before the Doctor and waited. The Doctor looked at it and shook his head. "Eighty-three days on moss," he murmured. "Eighty-three days!" After a time he picked up the glass. He lost the first two swallows and passed out again. The next two he kept down. After that, little by little, his stomach began to accept food.

Pete got part of the tragic story on the way back to Cordova. They had hiked across the mountains as he had figured. The kid had died of starvation two weeks after the hike. "All he talked about those last days was Captain Pete," the Doctor said. "I'd steer him onto his family and home in

the States but in a minute he'd be back on Captain Pete."
The Doctor had kept the body in the second cabin and once
a day had doused it with ice water to retard decomposition.

Before Pete arrived, Dr. Allberry figured he had two or
three days at most left. He never did tell Pete, or anyone,
why they went to Montague Island or why they hiked across
the mountains to Nellie Martin River. Pete found one thing
more that added to the mystery when he visited their first
camp at McLoud Harbor later. It was a box, more than a foot
square, filled with flashlight batteries. There were enough to
last a couple of years.

What happened to Dr. Allberry? After Pete returned him
to Cordova he simply disappeared.

"The one thing that really hurt me," Pete said, "was what
Al Tibbett had written in a little notebook I found on the
cabin floor. He had written in words so shaky I could hardly
make them out, 'Pete will come for me, but it'll be too late,' "
Pete shook his head. "He was a real nice kid."

I thought of Pete's words to the little old man this morning
as he had given him a few spuds, milk and butter to tide him
over until the next trip: "Suppose something happened to me
and the *Siren*. You'd starve." And the old man's confident
answer, "Oh, you'll get through all right."

I thought of the girl, Betty, holding up her baby, saying
happily, "He's gained three pounds," and of the old woman
alone—"If anything happens, Pete will take care of us." The
happy boarders at Chenega, and Al Tibbett's hope in the face
of certain death seemed to express a common thought.

Pete knew how to say it. "When the *Siren* comes it's almost like God."

11

I Meet the Octopus

Every denizen in the sea gets into the fish trap. The day I met my first octopus, I was down inspecting the heart of the Seven Sisters Trap when I came suddenly on him not ten feet away. He hung to the wire, gripping it with spread-out tentacles, looking like a giant spider in the gloom. His black eyes were watching me and I had the feeling he was poised, waiting for my next move. He was not big—maybe five or six feet. But he was an octopus. I took one look and shot for the surface.

Thinking it over afterward I realized this meeting had been inevitable and in all probability there would be many more of them.

With this thought in mind I set about gathering all the information possible about him. Somewhere there may be a great deal of information on the octopus, but it is certainly not easily available, and I did not find it. What I did find were some written and word-of-mouth accounts by a handful of divers, professional and amateur, and scarcely more than sketchy descriptions of their frightening encounters with him.

I did learn that long before man braved the depths in the first crude diving suit the octopus was well established as the terror of the deep. He is, without doubt, the world's ugliest, most repulsive creature, and hasn't a friend on earth or in the sea.

The octopus is a solitary, sulking individual who shuns all company. He lurks in rock crevices, caves and old wrecks, and his cold, emotionless eyes stare bleakly out at the diver and all sea life. His eight suction-studded tentacles lie coiled and waiting to dart out and clamp onto his victim. He is the Frankenstein monster of the deep. He is Mr. Repulsive in person, more hideous and forbidding the thousandth time than the first.

I found little concerning his strength and speed, his manner of fighting, or the way I should fight or avoid him. The few divers who had fought him all seemed to have come on him suddenly and were attacked by the octopus. The fights had always consisted of wild slashings with a knife at gripping tentacles or stabbing at the octopus with a spear. In almost every case the diver escaped without killing the octopus. I found not one factual case of a diver being killed by an octopus.

I did discover that even his manner of eating is on a par with his looks. His main diet is crab. Once captured, the victim is bitten by the parrotlike beak, and a digestive juice is forced into its body from the octopus' mouth. This juice paralyzes the victim, then dissolves and partly digests the flesh, the resulting soup being sucked back into the octopus' mouth.

I found, too, that some of the world's largest octopuses inhabit Alaskan waters. Spread out they have been known to measure in excess of twenty-eight feet.

With only this inadequate knowledge of his size and my limited diving experience, I knew that to wait until we came face to face beneath the sea could prove fatal. So I went out on my own to learn firsthand the things I needed to know. I went to the octopus himself.

Near Halibut Point, at Sitka, there is a stretch of clear, rock-strewn bottom that is perfect for an octopus. When the tide is out, stranded young octopuses crouch in countless shallow pools that pock the shore. It was here, with a twelve-foot pole, that I went to school.

Pike pole in hand I would move among the pools peering into shadowy holes and crevices. I would look for a tentacle stretched snakelike along the face of a rock, a pair of coal-black eyes watching me from between two rocks, a pinkish pear-shaped mass crouched far back in a hole.

When I found one I moved in, spear ready. He never came out at me, but crouched far back watching with a stare that in itself was disconcerting. When I gigged him he immediately began waving his eight tentacles in wild confusion. The moment one came in contact with the pike pole he grabbed and yanked. One or two more arms would pop out and join the first. With the others he anchored to bottom and began to pull, or more likely, just held on.

Unless I was braced the first yank of a four- or five-foot octopus took me off my feet or ripped the pike pole free. When he settled down to hanging on, his strength was a match for mine. On more than one occasion I had to kill him to rescue it. The best and quickest way to kill an octopus is to drive the pike pole through the soft, fleshy head just above and between the eyes.

I graduated from the Halibut Point beach school to the open sea in a hurry. I was not ready to face the big ones. I doubt that any diver is ever ready. But there were other questions I wanted answered and only the big fellows could do that. Would they, too, be reluctant to come out of a hole; would they deliberately attack a diver, lying in wait for him, as picture and story had them doing? What would happen to the diver if one got close enough to wrap a few tentacles around him? And suppose he got the diver helpless, completely wrapped up in tentacles? I got part of the answer off Cape Edgecumbe, in the open sea. I got some more of it in almost every trap I dove, for the octopus, like all other sea life, got into the traps. But for the ultimate test—the answer to that fateful last question—I had to wait. Eventually it came.

Having these unanswered questions hanging over me each time I dove was ten times more nerve-racking than hunting brown bear. With the bear I was reasonably sure what to expect and prepared for it. I was hunting him on land, an environment in which I, too, was at home. And I carried the most modern, high-powered weapon available.

With the octopus I was challenging the ugliest creature in the sea, a creature of tremendous strength and a disposition reputed to be sly and deadly. I would be meeting him in a foreign world that in itself held certain death for me in a thousand ways. Half my thoughts must be continually occupied with the mechanical necessities of just keeping alive below. My movements would be ponderous and slow, my sight limited to a few gloomy feet. My weapon would be almost as old as man—a knife with a blade a foot long that I made from a saw, or a spear I fashioned by cutting off the barb of a pike pole and shortening the shaft to six feet. The knife went with me on all dives. I preferred the spear but it was awkward to handle. The only time I took it down was when I knew I was in octopus-infested waters.

The open sea beyond Cape Edgecumbe is a favorite breeding ground for octopuses. The water is clear, the bottom rocky. I was called to Cape Edgecumbe to try to recover a ten-ton anchor that had been lost among the rocks during a storm.

I was down about seventy feet, carrying the spear, and stumbling and creeping through a rock quarry of stones from the size of marbles to four-room houses. There were crevices and caves on all sides, perfect homes for octopuses. But even here there was a housing shortage. There were thousands of octopuses out in the open. Little fellows, like great spiders, no more than nine inches across, were spread out on rocks as though sunning themselves. Their bigger brothers and sisters clung to other rocks or sat upright on the floor of the sea.

As I approached they shot off in all directions. Some zoomed out ahead to disappear into the clear liquid distance. Others popped straight up in front of me, or shot off to right and left, like quail frightened out of long grass by the hunter's feet. I was so conscious of those octopus swarms about me that I could have stumbled over that ten-ton anchor and not seen it.

The little fellows were first to leave. The larger the octopus the slower he was in moving. A six-footer would pop up, squirt off a few feet with tentacles streaming, settle on bottom and sit glaring malevolently as I passed.

The octopus has two means of locomotion. Normally he moves along bottom on three or four tentacles. Several may be coiled against his body and the rest trailing like so many tails. For speed he possesses the original jet-propulsion motor. He propels himself forward in surprisingly swift jerks by sucking water through vents on either side of his head where it passes through gills and is ejected with terrific force.

I had progressed about a hundred yards when I met my first big fellow. I squeezed between two rocks and came upon him sitting in the open, not more than twenty feet away and staring at me with cold, expressionless eyes. I guessed that, spread out, he measured a good twelve feet. He sat facing me, propped on three tentacles. One trailed out behind, the rows of suckers plainly visible. The rest were coiled tight against his body.

I stopped, unable to suppress a shudder, not from fear, but from the sheer repulsive look of him. At that moment I understood why all the fearsome tales that have been laid at his door through the centuries have passed as unquestioned fact. He has the size and looks to lend credence to man's most fantastic story of octopus terror beneath the sea.

We looked at each other a few seconds. Then he began moving off on his three tentacles in the most leisurely manner. Suddenly, as if jerked by a string, he shot away and wedged himself into the crevice between two rocks. I walked carefully by, gripping my spear, making no overt moves, but I sensed his eyes following me. I sensed them long after I was out of the water.

I had my first nose-to-nose meeting with an octopus while inspecting the lead at Red Head Trap. A trap lead half to three quarters of a mile long is too far to walk on bottom. So

I use a special trick that saves both time and strength. I sink halfway down the depth of the lead and lying out flat, pull myself forward hand over hand by hooking my fingers through the wire mesh. This way I can travel as fast as a man can walk and do a good job of inspecting. A lot of seaweed had drifted in and was held against the lead by the tide. I zoomed along, parting the seaweed with one hand and shooting through. I had covered more than half the distance when I burst through a clump and came face to face with the biggest octopus I have ever seen. I figured later that he had become tired bucking the current and was resting against the wire. His tentacles were curled close and the sea bounced him against the lead gently as a beach ball. His body was big as a fifty-gallon drum; the tentacles next to his body looked almost a foot thick. I guessed his spread at better than twenty feet. I saw, as through a magnifying glass, the pinkish, fine-textured skin, tough tentacles and row on row of saucer-shaped suckers.

My left hand, reaching for a pull, was about to land like a prize fighter's jab between his eyes. I killed the punch and stopped my forward motion in nothing flat. My heart, stomach and everything inside piled into my throat. A tentacle unfurled lazily, then I hit the chin valve, releasing the air in the suit, and plunged to bottom. I scrambled along bottom fast for perhaps fifty feet, then turned and looked back. I did not see him again.

I felt no fear, as you normally feel fear. But it was there, buried beneath bone-deep revulsion at his hideous appearance. I can understand how a diver might lose all reason and the ability to fight back or think, when a tentacle unexpectedly snakes out to imprison an arm or leg.

The fact that he did not follow made me think he shot away as the others had, for this was open sea. What he might do in the confines of a cave or sunken ship that he considered home was another matter. Sunken ships are a favorite haunt of the octopus. A good deal of a diver's work consists of raising sunken ships, if that operation is practicable, or of salvaging valuable equipment.

The old seiner was a good example. She hit a rock in a dense fog, ripped out her bottom and sank so quickly there was barely time for the crew to toss over a skiff and jump. Everything was lost, including several thousand dollars locked in the skipper's trunk behind the galley stove.

They hired me to salvage the trunk. The skipper and a crewman went along to tend air and telephone lines.

She was easy to find with the rock pinnacle she had hit for a marker. She lay in about sixty feet of water, tipped partially on her side. There was a huge splintered hole in her bow. I climbed aboard the sloping deck, edged through the wheelhouse, went down a couple of steps and through another door into the galley. It was a gray day with no sunlight to filter into the depths. The galley lay in deep gloom, the only light coming from two small ports that at sixty feet shone only as pale disks. I felt along the bulkhead, found the stove, ran my hands across its clammy top and located an opening that led to the back. I leaned in, groping, felt the end of a box, found a handle and began to pull. It was almost clear when I had the prickly sensation I was being watched. To understand that feeling on the ocean bottom—imagine yourself in a haunted house on the blackest night. You know no living soul has entered this place in a hundred years—but as you creep through the eerie dark you suddenly feel eyes following you, and are conscious of another presence. I dropped the trunk, turned, and stood staring into the gloom around me.

Then I saw him—rather, I saw the vague, pear-shaped outline with four or five coiled tentacles. He was pulled back into the farthest corner of the galley, but was still less than eight feet from me. His outline looked as big as the one at Red Head Trap.

I stood motionless, looking back at him. My first thought was, "Where are those other tentacles?" Would I suddenly feel a powerful yank at arms or legs? Almost unconsciously I braced myself.

In a way I had him cornered. He had to pass within a foot of me to get out. He also had me trapped. There was little room to swing a knife in this close space and with such darkness I would be stabbing at a shadow. If he tried to escape there was my air line coming through the door. He might snag it, rip it loose from the suit and leave me stranded here. I stealthily unscrewed the knife from the scabbard and left it hanging free for a quick snatch. I needed both hands to gather up my air line and telephone line; I was getting out. This had to be done quickly, carefully, smoothly, so as not to excite him.

Air was building in the suit; in a moment I would float. But a sudden burst of released air might frighten him into attacking or trying to escape. I put my chin against the valve, barely cracking it. A thin stream of bubbles leaked out and trickled through the door into the sea. The octopus remained quiet.

I stepped backward, was reaching for the first coil of hose when it happened. There was no tip-off, like a cat's crouch, a bird's spring as it takes flight. One instant he was still, cowering, the next he exploded out of the corner. I reached for the knife, but before I touched it, he was on me— There was a whip of tentacles past the face plate. A stream of expelled water slammed me backward against the trunk and stove. I caught one glimpse of him shooting through the door. He completely filled the opening. There was a sharp, scraping drag along the air line, then I was alone.

I sat down on the trunk, feeling sick and shaky. After a little I got some starch in my legs again, hauled the trunk outside and floated to the surface with it. At the moment I was satisfied if I never saw another octopus and I certainly wanted no more tests.

As it happened, a diver named Scotty Evans made the final test that proved the creature's viciousness. Evans, a big fellow and a good diver, was in Alaska without a suit and for a time we joined forces on outside jobs and took turns diving. One of those jobs took us back to Cape Edgecumbe, the octopus-infested rock quarry I had dived before. We were going to have another look for the ten-ton anchor. For help we had a big-shouldered Swede who was going halibut fishing soon and a wiry little fellow named Jerry. Jerry was supposed to know the anchor's location, having been a watchman on the trap the season it ripped loose. Ten-ton anchors are unusual in the North and this one was especially valuable. It had been used to hold a floating trap against a particularly tough rip tide. If we found it there would be no trouble selling it back to the cannery for six or seven hundred dollars.

I went down first. Evans was on the telephone and Swede on the air line. It was a warm, bright day, without a cloud. Seventy feet down I could still see the shadow of the boat's bottom through the clear water. I had decided that in this open sea there should be no trouble with the octopuses, so I left the spear on deck. The same swarms of big and little octopuses began taking off in all directions again. I crawled about through this boulder field for two hours and found nothing.

When I came up Evans donned the suit. He wanted a life line so we fastened a three-quarter rope about him. His diving experience had been around docks in harbors; he had never seen an octopus. "You'll see a lot of them down there but just go ahead about your business," I told him. "If you come across a big one that doesn't take off immediately, wait a minute. He'll leave."

The octopuses surprised and startled him. At first he was constantly saying excitedly, "There goes a big devil! There goes another! Man, oh man!" Finally the novelty wore off and I heard no more. For an hour we crept back and forth across the sea on a course Jerry set. Then Evans said, "There's a big old granddaddy down here in a hole. If Swede wants him for halibut bait send down a spear."

"You bet I want him," Swede said. "Octopus arms are the best bait there is."

I fastened a shackle to the spear and dropped it into the sea.

A minute later Evans' voice sang out, "One octopus coming up." Then silence—silence shattered by a blood-chilling scream. The air and life lines began jerking madly and the terrified screaming went on and on in my ears.

I yelled, "Haul him up, quick!"

Jerry and Swede began yanking on the life line.

I shouted into the phone, "Evans, what's wrong? What happened?"

The only answer was that wild, hysterical screaming. There was but one explanation. Something had misfired, and seventy feet down Scotty Evans was fighting for his life with the octopus. Swede and Jerry could not lift him. I added my strength and still we could not budge him off the ocean floor.

Jerry and Swede held the strain and I returned to the telephone. I had to break through Evans' fear somehow. Only by understanding the situation below would we know what to do. I began talking to him, repeating the same words over and over.

"We're trying to help you, Evans! But you've got to tell me what happened. You've got to tell me, understand? Tell me! Tell me!"

I don't know how often I repeated that before I made out his first half-sobbing words, "He's got me! Oh, God, he's got me!"

The moment he began talking he quieted down and talked sanely.

Evans had found the octopus in a hole under a ledge. His aim had been poor and he had driven the spear low-down into the body. The octopus ripped it from his hands, shot out a pair of tentacles and wrapped them about his leg. Evans had drawn his knife but in his frantic struggle had lost it before he could cut himself free. Then we had tightened on the life line. Now we were hauling on him from one end and the octopus from the other. We held our strain, the octopus held his.

We needed another diver to go down and kill the octopus but I knew of none in Alaska. So we held our strain and tried to think. Swede said, "Why not lower the anchor right over him with Evans directing us, and drop it on him. Maybe we can kill him or make him let go."

I relayed this to Evans. "We're both under the rock shelf. You'd miss us ten feet."

Jerry said, "We've got another pike pole we can send down." But the shelf would keep that from Evans too.

We were out of ideas and utterly helpless. I ran up a distress flag hoping another boat would come by and help us. We took a pass around a cleat with the life line, putting all the strain on Evans' leg we dared—and waited. A half hour crawled away. I asked, "Scotty! How are you doing?"

"My leg's numb." His voice was thin and sharp. "I can't hold out much longer. Virg, what are we going to do?"

"How hard did you stick him with the spear?" I asked.

"Pretty hard. Why?"

"Maybe he'll weaken soon and have to let go."

"If he don't, then what?" he asked again.

"There'll be a boat along any minute. We'll get some help."

"What good is help up there?"

"Wait and see," I said. "Just don't lose your nerve." But he was right. A hundred men up here would not help.

An hour dragged away. The steady *pop, pop* of the compressor was the only sound. The sea stayed calm and empty. The sun streamed down. Seventy feet away, on the end of the line we held, a man's life was running out. I searched the horizon for a boat until my eyes ached and sky and sea ran together. I kept up a steady run of talk to Evans.

A second hour passed.

I filled the compressor with gas. We held our strain; the octopus held his. Every few minutes now, Evans asked in an increasingly sharp voice, "You see a boat yet? Why in hell don't you see a boat? How many hours I been down? It seems like years." Then he would add, "God! this guy is big. What—what happens if he gets at me? Does he use that beak?"

"Cut it out," I said sharply. "We're going to get you out." I looked at the taut life line disappearing into the depths and searched the empty sea for sign of a boat.

We waited—and waited.

Suddenly Evans was half sobbing, "I can't stand no more. I can't stand it! There's no boat coming. Even if one did they can't do a thing. I'm out of luck. . . ."

It is a terrible thing to be so close, so helpless, and hear a man crack up.

I said, "You're crazy. You're yellow. You haven't the guts to fight it out." I called him everything. He could not get in a word. Finally the sobbing stopped.

After a little he said quietly, "All right, Virg. All right." I sat down on the rail and looked at my feet. I could not look at Swede or Jerry and I did not once glance at the sea.

We waited again—and waited.

Then Evans' voice said, "Virg, I've thought it out. I figured like you at first. That he would get sick from the sticking and let go. But he ain't. Maybe he can hold me here for days. Anyhow, I know there ain't much gas left for the compressor. When that runs out I'm done. Only a diver can help me and there's no diver. I've got one chance, just one. Start the boat and begin pulling."

"We'd pull a leg off," I said.

"I know that." The fatalistic calm of his voice made my skin crawl. "I don't want to be left down here with an octopus. Start pulling! You'll get most of me."

Swede shook his head when I told him. "He knows what he wants."

Jerry wiped his sweating face. He looked at the water, around the empty horizon. "Maybe—maybe if I ease her in slow—take just a little pull—"

"Scotty," I said into the telephone, "we're going to try a pull with the boat. I want you to tell me exactly how it goes. Exactly, understand?"

"Pull!" he said. "Start pulling!"

The engine started. Jerry glanced at me, at Swede; his face was tight, shiny. He eased in the clutch. The propeller bit into the water. The boat moved forward. The life line crept aft. Strain came into it. "Scotty," I asked, "how is it going?"

The phone was dead. Then the line was swinging forward to straight down. It could mean but one thing. Evans' voice croaked, "Virg! Virg! I'm coming up!"

I yelled and jumped for the life line. Jerry cut the motor. The three of us hauled in like mad. Evans was coming up under the boat. He was ready to break the surface before we fought him clear. It was not the diving helmet that rose above the sea, but the ugly pear-shaped body of a giant octopus. He was perched atop the helmet, all eight tentacles twined about Evans' body. I grabbed the pike pole and with a single smash drove it, spur and all, completely through his head and a yard beyond.

We got the helmet off and stripped away the suit. He had been sick inside the helmet several times. He stretched out on deck, eyes shut, and drew in great gulps of air. The octopus had held him on bottom for three hours.

At last he muttered, "That pull broke him loose, then he climbed on top of me. I—I thought I was a goner then."

An hour later he was all right. His left leg was sore a couple of days but that was all.

Evans' experience proves something I have thought a long time. Part of the diver's trouble with the octopus is panic when he is grabbed. Another is the diver's provoking the creature into attacking. This octopus would not have attacked Evans had he not speared him.

I have often had a pair for company while working fifty or a hundred feet down inside a trap. But the octopus is no salmon eater if anything else is available, so an armed truce exists between us. He keeps as far from me as possible, always moving away along the wire or crawling off across bottom, always watching me, giving the impression he is set to spring. I go about my business keeping at least one eye on him and making no warlike moves.

His strength was fully demonstrated that day. We found later, on examination, that Evans had stuck the creature well, yet he had held the diver down three hours against the combined pull of three big men. As for his fighting ability, old time whalers have told me of finding deep scars inflicted by octopuses on the heads of captured sixty-ton whales. That is good enough for me.

12

Fortune Hunting

Like every diver since diving time began I went
through the "hunting for treasure" period, with visions of
fortunes waiting to be torn from rotting hulks beneath the
sea. The visions were brightened by stories of sunken ships
whose barnacle-encrusted safes were reputedly bursting with
gold dust from the early stampede fields. Discounting the dust
these sunken ships were still valuable salvage. Even military
vessels, coastal schooners and tramps have currency aboard.

All some diver had to do was find them, I reasoned. They
had not been found because Alaska was a new frontier not
blessed with people, especially not with divers searching for
sunken treasure.

One of the first treasure stories I heard was a yarn that to
this day fascinates me. Like so many that are impossible to
check, it was fantastically plausible from a diver's point of
view. It seemed that years ago a ship had gone down with a
reported cargo of almost a million dollars in dust aboard. She
was located lying in two hundred and fifty feet of water. Too

167

deep, the insurance company believed, to make a salvage operation successful. She was written off as a total loss.

Years later a pair of divers stumbled across her and decided to try to reach the safe. The insurance company discovered their operation and ordered them to stop.

The company, now convinced salvage was possible, hired the two divers and half a dozen others, then set up their own salvage operation. When they finally reached the safe it was empty.

Each year since, the two original divers, outfitted with sluice boxes, a boat and an immense sucker hose, pull out into the sea a mile off a certain point. There they set up the sluice boxes on deck. One diver goes below with the sucker and begins pulling a stream of sand and silt from the bottom into the sluice boxes. In a few weeks they remove enough gold to keep them in luxury the remainder of the year.

They insist they have found a gold mine, one hundred feet down on sea bottom. "If you don't believe it, come out and put on the suit. Go down and look at our claim stakes," they say.

What seems more logical is that they somehow took the gold from the wreck right under the insurance company's nose and transferred it to a safer hiding place in Davy Jones's locker.

Then there is the story of the old wooden steamship *City of Portland*. Years before she had sunk in a storm somewhere off Bligh Reef. There was talk of a big gold shipment aboard. An engineer on an Ellamar Cannery tender had seen the wreck of an old wooden ship off Bligh Reef. But his location directions were vague.

I did find two wrecked ships on Bligh Island. One must

have met disaster a hundred years ago. She was a Russian sailing vessel about a hundred and twenty feet long. The hand-hewn keel and ribs, fastened with great, square, hand-forged nails, is all that remains. Gray and weather-stained, she sits high and dry, half buried in the beach sand. I have landed often, walked about among her ribs and speculated on her cargo and crew, the manner of her wrecking. I dug in the sand and unearthed several old buckles and a few pieces of rusty iron. She sits a hundred feet from the water and is a good six feet above the highest tide. It must have been a grand-daddy of a storm that put her there.

The second ship, a few miles distant, was a modern Jap freighter. She lay submerged to her rusted superstructure, her crushed bow hard against the rocks that sank her. I dove her once in the hope of salvaging brass fittings, valves, pipe and tools. But another diver had beat me to her.

I ran down a number of gold salvage stories, only to learn there were insurmountable obstacles. But I was never discouraged. With so many stories, I was convinced that eventually a good one had to come along. It was just a matter of waiting and keeping my eyes and ears open.

In the meantime, I had learned there is other salvage work in Northern waters than the search for sunken gold-bearing ships. Literally hundreds of boats have been lost in this land of blinding fogs and sudden storms. Divers have been known to clean up small fortunes salvaging equipment or raising boats.

The crew of an eighty-foot tender went on a celebration in Valdez. After a wild night they pulled out, still celebrating. Well out in the Sound they pointed her nose for home, set her on automatic pilot, then the crew passed out to a man.

For three hours the boat plowed down the Sound, then a rock came up dead ahead.

When the crew shook the drugged sleep from their eyes, they were swimming. Miraculously not a man was lost. Later, when I extended my sympathies to the skipper over the loss of his fine boat, he said, "Why, we had only drifted off course a half mile."

The tender was later raised and towed into harbor. The salvor's fee was six thousand dollars.

Another diver I knew of had raised a seiner that had been sunk only two months. He spent some time and a little money cleaning her up. Then he ran her to Seattle and sold her for twenty thousand.

My beginning as a salvor was anything but auspicious.

A machinist lost a kit of tools in Cordova Harbor. He had tripped and fallen while going aboard the boat one night. Several weeks later I heard the story from a pair of fishermen in the Alaska Bar. The tools, they insisted, were worth at least five hundred. I was sure I could resell them for at least half that amount. So next day I hired a local fellow for ten dollars to tend lines and made the dive.

I landed almost on top of the tools and began fishing them out of the mud. They consisted of a double handful of old knuckle-buster wrenches, part of a set of rusty sockets strung on a wire. There were a few open-end wrenches, a half-dozen files and several machine hammers. The mess was worth about twenty dollars to anyone hard up for tools. I dumped them behind the wood box in the Western Fisheries *Number 9* and forgot them.

I had learned my first disillusioning lesson. The value of most salvage multiplies at least ten times in the telling.

Practically everyone had a favorite salvage story and I heard it the moment they learned I was a diver. The problem was to separate fact from fiction, then to nail down an approximate value to see if a search was worth while.

Hardy Kane, who owns a fish trap and pile driver, told me of an old windjammer loaded with tin bar for the canneries. She had sunk long ago off Port Etches. A check showed her to be well within diving range, and the tin would be worth a fortune now. But tin bar is heavy and the Port Etches bottom is soft mud. The bar might have sunk into the mud a hundred feet and be impossible to find.

One night, while lying at the cannery dock, I dropped into the galley of the *Northern Queen* for a cup of Johnny Harris' good coffee. Johnny was short and stocky. He had served two of his Army years in the North.

We sat at one end of the table with our coffee. The pot boiled on the back of the great stove. The aroma of cooked food still hung in the warm air. Johnny said, "Had a miner for dinner the other day. All he could talk about was, if he could just get a tractor. Made me think of the two the Army brought into Resurrection Bay." Listening to tales of his Army life was the price I always paid for Johnny's coffee and doughnuts. As usual I now listened with one ear while, through the open door, I watched the sun fall behind the line of peaks across the Sound. Night shadows faded over the water turning it darker and darker. The noisy sea gulls had settled for the brief night along the cannery ridge and the dock railing. The distant bunkhouse windows were yellow in the twilight.

Then I heard Johnny say, ". . . and both them tractors rolled right off the barge into ninety feet of water. If a man could raise them I bet they would be worth plenty up here to guys like that miner."

"What was that?" I asked.

"Ain't you been listening?" he wanted to know.

"I was thinking of something else," I confessed. "What was that about tractors?"

"The Army was bringing in these two R.D. 8 tractors on a flat barge. When we came into Resurrection Bay a big wave tilted the barge and the tractors ran over the blocks into the sea."

"Good tractors?"

"Brand new."

"You know where they are?"

"Man, I was on that barge. I can go right to the spot. But you could never get them up. Those tractors weigh twenty-five tons each."

"And worth twenty-five thousand each," I said. "They can be raised. I know where I can rent a floating crane. Those tractors weren't running, so the motors probably aren't damaged. Cleaned up, I'll bet we can sell the two for twenty or thirty thousand to the miners around Fairbanks. But we'll have to make one inspection dive before ordering the crane." I was beginning to get excited.

Johnny edged forward on the bench. "You really serious, Virg?"

"You don't kid about twenty thousand," I said. "You want to try for it?"

"I can get away Saturday and Sunday," Johnny said.

"We'll start early. I'll pick you up about five."

"Fifty-fifty if we raise them," he said.

"Fifty-fifty." We shook hands on it.

Resurrection Bay is big. It is surrounded on three sides by mountains. Johnny took us to a spot about a mile off the rocky shore, got his bearings from several points on the beach, and dropped the anchor. "Right down there." He pointed over the side. "You should land right on them."

We got the diving ladder over the side and I climbed into the suit. We were both getting excited. "Know what I'm going to do with my half that dough?" he said. "I'm going to open a restaurant in Anchorage. Man, I'll be rolling in dough in no time."

"I'll go back to Idaho and set myself up in the electrical business," I said. "There is only one good electrician in the county."

Johnny was ready to set the helmet on, when there was a shout across the water and an Army boat loaded with soldiers and bristling with guns bore down on us.

"What do you think you're going to do, mac?" a burly sergeant demanded.

I explained about the tractors and said I was going to try to recover them.

"That's what we figured when we seen this diving outfit. Those tractors are the property of the U.S. Army, mister."

"Those tractors are lost. They're free salvage now," I pointed out.

"They belong to the Army," he repeated. "Now beat it."

"The Army will never raise them and you know it," I said. "What's wrong with me doing it?"

"I didn't come out here to argue, mac. I came to tell you to beat it. Now get going."

Johnny hauled up the anchor, swearing under his breath, and we headed back for Cordova.

The tractors are still there, twenty or thirty thousand dollars' worth—only ninety feet under water.

The time between dives is often one of utter monotony. I check equipment, clean up the boat, then wander the streets and visit the bars. Cordova is two blocks long and supports four bars. During the week, while everyone is fishing, I am often the only man on the street, the bartender and I the only ones in the bar.

One day to vary this routine I left *Number 9* tied to the dock and went aboard a tender for the run to several traps. The tender was an old ferry from a small Washington coastal town. It had been reconverted for tender service in Alaska.

Returning that night, fog closed down tight and thick. We were feeling our way somewhere between Goose Island and the cannery. I was standing in the galley door staring into the white wall, thinking what a spot this would be in a small boat without a compass, when there was a thunderous explosion and tongues of flame leaped out the engine-room door and windows. The motor, an old gas burner, had backfired through the carburetors spewing gas in all directions.

There was no chance to fight it. We tossed over a skiff, piled in and pulled away fast before the gas tanks exploded.

We lost the tender in a dozen strokes and gradually the crackle of flames died away. We were suddenly five big men in an open dory, lost in the eerie closeness of fog, rowing blindly into a silence broken only by the click of oarlocks, the faint dripping of water.

After a little, one of the boys said, "We're going wrong. We're heading for the open sea."

"No," the skipper said. "We pulled off in the same direction we were heading. We're all right."

We might have been rowing in circles for all I knew. I was lost.

We took turns rowing, moving steadily through the fog, trying to hold a straight course. There was little talking, but I could guess we were all thinking the same thing. No one knew our exact location when the fire broke out, so we could be hours out here. Suppose the wind came up and this calm sea started to build. The first wave would swamp this over-loaded dory.

Some time later the faint sound of a bell pierced the silence. We knew where we were then and tension ran out of us. An hour later, following the voice of the bell, we rowed into Cordova's harbor.

The boys immediately headed for the Alaska Bar, where in typical sailor tradition, we began celebrating our miraculous deliverance from the sea.

We told everyone, and each other over again, what a terrific explosion it had been, how the flames raced and roared. We gave stroke-by-stroke descriptions of the four- or five-mile row in, of how close, and the number of times, we had almost gone wrong.

I kept thinking, there had been no second explosion. That meant the motor, a lot of valves and electrical equipment could be salvaged. I could sell most of it back to the cannery. The salvage should amount to at least five thousand dollars. We had been right on course. She should not be hard to find. I would start looking for her as soon as the fog lifted in the morning.

A man came into the bar and asked, "Say! what boat were you guys on?"

Someone told him. He said with dream-shattering blunt-ness, "Your boat just drifted into the harbor with the tide."

We returned to the dock and there she was, riding calmly out in the channel. An inspection revealed that the only damage was a few broken windows and scorched paint. The fire had died after the spewed gas was consumed.

Such a fog once led a seiner to destruction when she struck a rock. The crew had managed to reach shore but were unable to give the owner an accurate location. The owner had leased the boat on a percentage. He now wrote off as a total loss. To any diver she was now free salvage. I talked with two of the crew members, trying to pin-point the spot where she had sunk. Each chose a different location. I dove both spots with no luck.

Several weeks later a pair of divers stumbled across her. I had passed directly over the sunken boat on the way to make my dives.

They raised the boat by sinking drums to her, then pumping them full of air. After towing her into dry dock they fell to, built a new bow, re-outfitted her and painted and calked all seams. They meant to fish her themselves.

The owner discovered this and sat back quietly, waiting. At last, after six months' work, when she was again ready for sea, and the partners were absent a few hours, he moved in with a sheriff and took possession. The partners walked away without a fight. One explained later, "We just figured some lawyer would get everything, so what was the use."

Charley Ryan, another diver, had better luck. He found his boat, a ninety-footer, high and dry on the ways, waiting for him.

I learned of it the night he came aboard while I lay at the

dock. "Virg," he said enthusiastically, "I bought the *Shepard Point* from the cannery."

I knew her well. When the cannery discontinued operations they left two boats sitting on the old ways. The *Shepard Point* was the largest. She had twin screws, twin engines and a gasoline starter engine. She had sat there rotting in the weather for two years. Her paint was peeled and the seams had opened up. I never tried but I was sure I could kick a hole through her bottom. "What can you do with her?" I asked. "She's not even worth salvage."

"Sure she is. I can fix her up, take her to the States, install new equipment and freeze clams for a cannery," he said grandly.

"Are you sure?"

"The deal is made. That's what I want to see you about. This is too big for one man. I'll sell you a half interest for fifteen hundred. We can make a killing."

I thought about it. But I kept seeing that peeling paint, the open seams, the rotten bottom. I did not have fifteen hundred to put into such a scheme. I told him so, adding, "I doubt if she floats when you launch. But if she does, she will never hold all that equipment you plan to put in."

"Wait and see. You're missing a chance," he said confidently.

Several days later he took on two partners. The three went to work on the *Shepard Point*.

I was in town on launching day and went down to help. Freshly painted and calked, the *Shepard Point* looked good, flanked by the deserted cannery on one side and the warped hulk on the other. Eighty feet of boat is a lot of boat. Even with rotten planking and old motors, if it floats and looks passable, it is worth something.

We greased the ways, knocked the blocks loose and she slipped into the sea. There we got the engines going and headed for the town's mooring basin. Almost immediately we noticed she was taking water fast in the engine room. The planks were floating and soon the engines would flood out. At this rate we would sink in a matter of minutes.

Before us stretched five miles of tide-flat beach without an obstruction. Ryan pointed her that way and slammed her aground.

We soon found our trouble. In addition to dozens of leaky seams the pipe that sucks in sea water to cool the motor had broken off and was flooding the compartment. We made repairs and were ready to go again. Then we discovered an amazing thing. We had not grounded on the beach. What we thought had been sea bottom was the top of an old railroad boiler, an abandoned part of the Copper River Railroad. It was the only thing on the beach bigger than a pebble. The weight of the boat had caved in the boiler to form a cradle that held her fast, balanced across the middle.

We dared not move for fear she would overbalance. So we waited, holding our breaths as the tide fell. Finally the boat perched high and dry above the sea and the water in the engine room drained out the cracks. The bow and stern bent like an inverted sickle, almost touching the mud. Each second we expected her to split in half.

After an age the tide turned and the ends rose with the sea. At full tide she floated. We backed off and again ran for the mooring basin. Once there Ryan said happily, "She's a darn good boat. She didn't bust. I told you she was, Virg. You missed a bet."

They eventually got her in shape and took off for the States. For a time nothing was heard.

Then one day I came in from Porcupine Trap and there was the *Shepard Point* tied in the basin. I tied behind her and went aboard. Ryan was in the galley. Over coffee he brought me up to date.

In the States they had installed twenty thousand dollars' worth of refrigeration equipment, after which they had taken on a huge load of clams. Then trouble began. They had to hold the clams aboard for lack of steamer space to ship them south. The insurance people became nervous, and eventually Ryan sold the clams to a cannery for enough to pay off the boat mortgage and they returned north. "It looked good. If we hadn't held those clams aboard so long and the insurance people hadn't become scared, we could have made it pay."

"What will you do now?" I asked.

"We've got all this equipment aboard and we can't sein her because she's over the legal length of fifty feet. She will never do for a tender." He scratched his head. "I guess we can fish halibut with her."

For a time they did well. Then one day, while lying at the dock with the starter motor running, the fuel line suddenly broke, spewing gas in all directions. Ryan leaped out of the engine room and ran. An instant later the spark on the running motor ignited the spraying gas.

The *Shepard Point* went up in a burst of flames. The only thing Ryan salvaged from his months of work was his diving suit.

The story of Charley Ryan and the *Shepard Point* would be

just another salvage operation gone wrong except that it illustrates an important point. In fortune hunting a man is often led through a circuitous, sometimes tortuous, chain of events to the pot of gold. When the *Shepard Point* went up in flames Ryan became desperate to recoup some of his losses. Always a salvor at heart with an eye out for a fast buck he was doubly so now. And he found it.

A week later when I came into the harbor, he was waiting for me on the dock. The moment he came aboard he said, "Virg, a scow load of six hundred cases of salmon capsized in a storm coming from the cannery at Kodiak. That load is worth at least ten thousand dollars, if we can find it before the sea eats through the tin."

"You're sure about this? You know where it is?"

"I talked with one of the tug's crew. The way he describes it, I've been past that point a hundred times."

Call it hunch, call it anything, but something told me not to let this one get away. "Okay," I said, "how soon do we go?"

My quick acceptance startled him and he asked, "You mean it? You'll go?"

"I can pull out in the morning," I said.

He grinned. "I'll get my diving suit aboard. You know, I've got a hunch about this one."

The point where the barge was said to have capsized was a long spear of rock thrust into a gray, choppy sea. The day was overcast, with a raw wind that roughed the sea and sent the gulls soaring.

Ryan made the first dive. He was down about three hours and found nothing. We moved to the opposite side of the point and I went down. For two hours I tramped the rocky bottom with no results. We spent a day taking turns diving in the vicinity. Finally Ryan said, "We might as well head back for Cordova. I'm lost now. We could dive here for a year and not find it." Pin-pointing a dive is of utmost importance. You never travel far under water and visibility is a few watery-gray feet.

Several nights later we were in Bob van Brocklin's Club Bar, in Cordova, trying to figure another way to get a line on the sunken barge. It was the middle of the week and we were the only customers. At the far end of the bar Van Brocklin finished dousing a half-dozen glasses, swiped a towel across the mahogany and drifted down to us. "You fellows look sick," he commented.

"We feel sick." Ryan told him of our search. "We've got to find it quick," he ended. "You know anybody that might give us a line on that salmon?"

"Sure," Van Brocklin said. "Me. I flew over the barge last week at low tide. You fellows were miles away." Van Brocklin owned a Piper Cub and had flown over most of Alaska and the Aleutians. A barge on bottom in clear water would be easy to spot.

"You can see that pile of salmon cases plain as day. There is an old wreck close by, too," he added. "In fact, I spotted the wreck first. When I went lower for a look at it I saw the salmon pile. At low tide the masts of this wreck almost stick out of water. There is a big rock just under the surface a few hundred yards off, where she must have hit. She's a wooden ship and she's been there for years. From what I could see of her and the location she must be the old first *Aleutian*. No other ship that size has sunk in those waters that I know of."

"The first *Aleutian!*" Ryan breathed. "Man, oh man! You hear that, Virg? The first *Aleutian!*"

"I heard him," I said. My heart had skipped a beat, then began to pound furiously.

Van Brocklin might as well have said he had found the Lost Dutchman Mine. The first *Aleutian*, the story goes, was returning to the States with an enormous gold shipment from the Nome and Fairbanks fields. She was caught in a raging storm, driven more than a hundred miles off course. Somewhere near Kodiak she struck a rock and sank in seven minutes. Certainly there was no time to remove anything of value.

"The light was just right that day to make her show up," Van Brocklin said. "I'll show you where she is, and that salmon, too, if you want to fly out tomorrow."

"Sure thing," Ryan said. "If we find anything you get a split."

"I'll take twenty-five per cent. Okay?"

"Okay," we both said. We shook hands on it. Then we had a drink to our future good fortunes, made a date to meet early next morning, and returned to the boat.

We lay in the dark cabin in our bunks. Cool night air funneled through the open port. I could feel the bump and scrape as the sea lifted us against the float. Ryan turned on his bunk, muttering, "Can't sleep. Excited, I guess."

"I know," I said.

After a moment he said, "I'll get another boat about the size of the *Shepard Point* and freeze clams again. It's a good deal if you have a good boat. I'll have the best. You want to come in this time?"

"I don't think so," I said.

"What will you do? What do you want most, Virg?"

I had never thought big before. Now I tried. From the time I had made my first dive I knew what I would like to do.

Reclaiming even a cheap kit of tools from the sea gave me a thrill nothing else could. And when I heard about a sunken ship I ran a fever. "I would like to be a salvor with enough equipment to go after big jobs," I said.

"You'll be able to," he chuckled.

"Maybe." I was suddenly assailed by doubts. "If it is the *Aleutian*. If that cargo of dust is really aboard."

"It's there," Ryan said. "I checked that long ago. And if Van Brocklin says it's the *Aleutian*, it is. Van is an old-timer, he knows these waters, and he never gets stampeded by a story. You can depend on anything he tells you."

"It still seems strange we should find her," I said.

"It probably seems strange to the guy who brings in an oil gusher, or the man who digs a million in dust out of a hole. I've seen it happen to people up here. At first most of them felt the way you do. They could not believe their luck. Well, somebody was bound to find the *Aleutian* someday. Why not us?"

"Okay!" I said. "I'm a salvor."

Morning brought a blustery day. Low scudding clouds swept across Eyak Mountain with a fine, driving rain.

The three of us took a cab to Eyak Lake, back of town, where Van Brocklin kept his plane. The plane was a two-seater. Van Brocklin could take but one passenger.

"You're the one to go," I said to Ryan. "You know these waters. I don't."

"All right. We should be back in a few hours. You be ready to pull out with the boat.' Ryan gripped my arm, his voice suddenly thick. "This is it, Virg. I got a hunch."

Van Brocklin grinned and waved crossed fingers. "See you soon, Virgil. Hold the fort."

I left them tinkering about the plane, preparing to take off, and returned to town in the cab. There I nervously paced the rain-wet streets. I thought of the two divers who had stumbled across the insurance job. We had stumbled, too, over six hundred cases of salmon and fallen headlong into a million in gold. I was no longer interested in a mere ten thousand dollars worth of fish. I was convinced that within a few hours we would be pulling out for Kodiak on the biggest, richest salvage job the North had known in years. It is hard to describe your feelings at such a time. I felt numb, as though I had been hit with a ball bat and had not fully recovered. At the same time every fiber of my body seemed stretched to the breaking point. Everything I ever wanted was crowding into my mind. I was walking about three feet off the ground and the world was a wonderful place to be in.

I turned into a restaurant and ordered a cup of coffee to kill time. "This is how it happens," I thought. "You look and look and draw a blank every time. Then, when you least expect it—*Boom!* the lightning strikes. Alaska—the land of golden opportunity."

A man burst through the door fairly shouting with excitement. "Bob van Brocklin just crashed on a take-off at Eyak Lake. He was killed."

I turned and looked at him. His words were a hammer hitting me in the stomach. They kept hitting me. The shock turned me sick and numb.

I sat, my fingers locked around the coffee cup, while his voice rushed on and on in the restaurant's stillness.

"Him and another guy took off. They got up about three hundred feet and the motor conked out. Then she took hold again. Van brought her around in a steep bank to set her down on the lake. She killed the second time right in the middle of the turn, and fell sideways into the lake. The passenger crawled out on a wing as she went down. Some guy on shore rowed out in a skiff, dived down and hauled Van out. His neck was broke."

A couple of waitresses and several customers had gathered around and were saying things about the crash, about Van Brocklin and the passenger. I remember that I finally asked if Ryan was all right. The man looked at me and said, "I couldn't tell. They took him to the hospital."

Then I walked out.

I went down the street and climbed the short hill to the little hospital. I met the doctor in the hall and asked how Ryan was.

"He's pretty badly bruised and has some minor cuts. He is also suffering from shock."

I asked if I could see him and the doctor said for only a couple of minutes.

Ryan's face was white and drawn with pain. "My hunch didn't pan out, Virg," he muttered.

"Forget it," I said. "We can still find it when you get out of here."

"Not a chance," he said. "It went with Van."

"Didn't he tell you where you were heading for when you took off?"

Ryan shook his head. "I didn't ask—didn't see any reason to ask. He was taking me there. Remember? The deal is dead, Virg. It's as dead as Van Brocklin."

The doctor came in and I left. I went down to the mooring

basin, walked along the deserted dock and stopped aboard *Number 9*. There were Ryan's diving dress and mine laid out side by side near the compressor. Everything was ready for the big dive. I stood there in the rain and looked at them.

13

Tales of the Whale

Chasing back and forth over the sea inspecting and repairing fish traps, it seems I see as many whales as seals and sea lions. That is not true, of course. But the whale is such a tremendous, awe-inspiring animal that the sight of him even a dozen or two times a day always stands out as an event.

Countless times I have run over the spot where one surfaced and disappeared, looked into the clear depths and thought, "He is down there, somewhere, a living animal twice the length and ten times the tonnage of this boat, holding his breath like a man, cruising about in that dim other world like a submarine." It is an eerie, skin-prickling thought.

Usually the most you see of a whale is a black section of long length curving gracefully out and into the sea again, the flirt of a broad tail sinking slowly from sight. But there are exceptions.

I was running the length of Knight Island Passage heading for the cannery at San Juan early one morning, when I witnessed a sight many old whaling men who have spent a lifetime at sea have not beheld.

It was one of those days you find too seldom in the North
—a kodachrome morning. The sky was cloudless. In the distance the white mountains circled the Sound. The sea lay flat
beneath the day's bright sunlight. The green shore line of
Chenega Island and the wide mouth of Whale Bay passed on
the starboard side. The curl of the bow wave and the *chuff-
chuff* of *Number 9*'s exhaust were the only sounds in the
world. I was off the tip of Squire Island when a silvery
streak shot out of the sea, a mile or so ahead. For one moment I thought it was a trick of sunlight on water. It came
again, wriggling, twisting upward, then falling back into the
sea. A leaping whale! One of the rarest sights a sailor can see.

I jerked the throttle wide and headed for the spot. I had
covered half the distance when I discovered there were two
whales and they seemed to be playing. One shot skyward
while the other lay on the surface like a log and pounded the
water with giant strokes of his tail.

At ten knots it seemed to take forever to reach them. When
I did the sea was again empty and calm. I cut the motor and
drifted. A few feet off a seal poked up his head without a
ripple and looked me over. A sea gull cried plaintively on the
distant shore. Minutes passed. Then several hundred feet off
the port, the sea heaved upward as if a mountain were emerg-
ing. A great black body, cascading sheets of water and foam,
shot spectacularly skyward. It hung a heart-stopping instant,
then toppled gravely sideways to be swallowed by the sea in
outflung blankets of green water. The second whale followed
immediately. He soared upward, shaking himself as though
trying to outdo the first. For a moment he seemed to walk on
his tail, then his giant bulk fell with a mighty splash.

I stumbled on deck with the camera, remembering I had

once read that a leaping whale had never been filmed. I focused on the spot and waited. Several minutes passed. Then a hundred yards away, on the opposite side of the boat, they went into the air together. They must have begun their rush toward the surface from tremendously deep and poured on the coal all the way. They rose straight up a good three-fourths their lengths, water cascading down their broad sides. Then they crashed back into the sea in a smother of foam, pounded their tails on the water with riflelike reports and rolled from sight. It all happened before I could focus and snap the camera. When next they surfaced they were a quarter mile astern and going away. All I got was a glimpse of black backs as they rolled sedately up and under.

Early in the season, I pulled into the Cedar Bay Trap for the inspection dive. The two watchmen and I were standing on the twelve-inch-wide trap walkway looking over the new wire before I went down. A whale came from out at sea. When we first noticed him he was a long black shadow barely under the surface, boring straight for the trap.

Whales often do that only to turn off, so we paid no attention. Then one of the watchmen yelled, "Hey! he's going to crash!" and wrapped both arms around a piling. The whale was not a hundred feet out, churning along full speed, showing no inclination to turn right or left. The other watchman and I snuggled up to respective pilings. We waited, holding our breaths, for the shock of his tons of weight crashing into the wire. He had drawn a bead on me. If he held his present course he would rip into the wire right at my feet. The piling I clutched would absorb a terrific shock.

We were ten feet above, looking down on him. I could see the measured lash of his broad tail driving him forward like

a battering ram. He was destruction on the loose, power un-
limited. He could wreck the trap, shake us into the sea with
him. Then what would happen?

I had a panicky thought to run, get away anywhere. But
there was no place to run except around the trap walkway.
So I hung tight to my piling and waited.

About fifty feet out he tipped downward and disappeared.
I estimated speed and distance and said to myself, "Now!"
and clung tight. Nothing happened. A couple of minutes later
he surfaced a hundred yards behind us, spouted and swam on.

We looked at each other, feeling foolish. One of the watchmen let out a breath and said, "Wire must not be down on
bottom. A hold-up."

"Must be," I said. "I'll take a good look. I got into the suit
and went down into the jigger. Some sixty feet down I circled the wire and found nothing. I entered the heart, went
halfway along one side, then suddenly fell another eighteen
or twenty feet before I hit bottom. A drop-off ledge began
in the middle of the heart and the wire, lying flat along the
first half of the bottom, left this drop-off ledge open. The
whale had sailed under the wire through this drop-off as
neatly as if he were the thread and the trap the needle. The
illustration on page 63 shows where he entered.

That was the only case I have ever known in which a whale
piled head on into a trap and did the cannery a favor.

Whales bring me a lot of work. When the watchmen see
them playing about near the trap they usually call me to look
over the trap again. He may have eased up and punched a ten-
foot hole through the wire. A ten-foot hole can empty a trap
teeming with fish in a few hours. Damage by whales, on the

whole, is unintentional. The big fellows blunder into the traps, become frightened and go crashing about. A full-grown whale on a rampage is the accumulated weight of a dozen big elephants running amuck.

I was passing the Port Chalmers Floating Trap one day when I saw the watchmen on the trap logs and turned in. Their appearance on the logs is often a signal they want to see me. As I drew nearer I saw that one of the boys held a rifle. I was still a couple of hundred yards off when he threw up the gun and fired. The sound slapped across the water. I looked and glimpsed the shine of a black back sinking from sight, following the lead toward the trap. A whale. The shots would be no more than pin pricks, but the sound might turn him.

Then the logs began to shake violently. The rifle flew from the shooter's hands into the sea. Both men dropped full length on the logs and lay flat. The whale had entered the jigger, gone into the heart, and torn out the side. He surfaced half-way between me and the trap. He charged half his length out of the sea with a rush, shaking his head like an angry bull, trying to dislodge a huge square of wire he had ripped out. It was stuck tight to his nose. He fell back with a tremendous splash, whirled and made for the trap again. The wire stuck to his nose and panicked him. I cut the motor, drifted, and watched. The watchmen clutched the heart logs, and waited.

The whale crashed through the side of the jigger with a heave of logs that almost spilled the men into the sea. He went through the heart, through the pot tunnel and tore out through the bottom of the pot, taking half the bottom and part of the side wall. The logs were heaving and tossing, wire

was squealing and ripping. The clinging men's yells were thin
and high. The whale took off for sea again, dragging yards of
wire with him. There were four ten-by-twelve-foot holes
and half the bottom of the pot was gone. The wreckage he
caused in less than a minute took me two days to repair and
the fish the cannery lost ran into thousands. No bulldozer
could have done as much damage in so short a time and I was
convinced no whale could possibly do more. I was wrong, as
Paddy Robinson can attest.

Paddy is a typical watchman, toughened by years at the
job. He could well serve as the trap watchmen's Paul Bun-
yan. But he is no mythical figure. At seventy he stands almost
six feet and weighs a tough one hundred and eighty pounds.
He can walk a trap log, pull an oar or swing a sledge with the
best of the young ones.

Paddy's Northern experience goes back half a century.
Name a job in the fishing industry, or in mining, and he has
likely held it. Listen to the most thrilling tales of the North
and you are sure to hear at least one about Paddy.

That season Paddy was watching alone aboard the Shelter
Bay Floating Trap. One afternoon he was sitting in the shack
drinking coffee when suddenly the cup jumped from his
hand, the chair upended, spilling him to the floor. The coffeepot crashed down beside him, showering him with hot coffee.
Pots and pans rattled off the walls and the canned goods
rained off the shelves. The shack groaned and the walls
swayed.

Paddy rushed outside, expecting to find a submarine earth-
quake piling up hundred-foot seas. What he saw was the
huge black head of a sixty-foot whale thrust up beneath

the shack and wrapped in yards of trap wire. The whale had come up under the trap, ripped through the bottom, charged halfway through and slammed his nose against the floor of the shack. As Paddy looked he backed down, then lunged powerfully upward to get free. He came completely out of water and fell half over the trap. He hung there, head down inside the pot. His great length was so balanced that he could not slide off and he could not raise his head high enough to breathe.

He began thrashing about. The great tail lashed out, ripped the planks from the walkway and hurled them into the sea. A smash caught the watchman's shack, splintered it to kindling and batted it after the planks. Paddy plunged into the sea to escape a like fate and clung shivering to the outside of the logs. The whale continued to pound the trap with giant strokes and beat the sea into foam. He set up a small storm inside the pot in his thrashing efforts to raise his head to breathe.

Paddy clung to the heaving logs. The cold water ate into his bones and numbed his body. The mad minutes dragged on. As the whale's breath slowly ran out, his efforts became wilder, more frantic. Then gradually they weakened. But many minutes passed before he was still. It took all Paddy's strength to pull his shivering body back onto the logs.

The trap was a wreck. The shack was gone, so was the skiff. There was no way to cross the more than quarter mile of sea to reach the shelter of the shore shack, and he was soaked. He spent a miserable night crouched in the lee of the dead whale, taking what shelter its body afforded from the chill night wind.

Next day when the cannery tender arrived, the whale still hung half in and half out of the trap. Paddy sat nonchalantly atop it, a butcher knife in hand, cockily giving the boat crew a "And what will you have, son, a bit of the white or dark meat?" look.

It took me three days to rewire the trap, while another crew built a new watchman's shack and repaired the walkway.

Several weeks later one of those sudden windstorms the Alaskans call williwaws boomed out of the Aleutians and caught me at sea. I ran for protection in Sleepy Bay, two miles distant. Sleepy Bay is a small, deep cup gouged out of the tip of Latouche Island. It remains calm during the worst blows.

By the time I had covered half the distance the waves were higher than the wheelhouse, their crests torn to sea smoke. One second *Number 9* stood on her stern as she climbed a mountainous sea, the next she was diving into a trough, heading straight for bottom. Tons of water crashed on the bow and raced the length of the deck. It took half an hour of fierce pounding to make the two miles.

The moment I entered the bay the sea flattened and the wind was gone. The storm was two thousand feet overhead where it was tossed by the island's high land mass. I had entered a vacuum of peace and quiet. I ran back the length of the bay and dropped the anchor. This storm could last hours, so I went into the galley, started the fire and put on the coffeepot. One thing you learn about this business is how to wait in comfort.

Suddenly the bulkhead jumped at me, pans rattled, the coffeepot tipped over, flooding the stove. I headed for the door, thinking another boat had run out of the storm and rammed me. I bounced on deck—then just stood there, my heart in my throat.

A huge, black, gleaming shape was rolling gravely out of the sea beside the boat, arching its body and going down again. A broad tail rose high as the cabin, waved languidly and sank beneath the sea. A hundred feet off, the same spectacle was being repeated. Dead ahead was another whale. Off the port side two whales rolled up, blew, and went down again in perfect unison. I counted twenty playing around me. Twenty!—like the ones who had wrecked Paddy's trap, who had torn the Port Chalmers Trap to ribbons.

My first thought was to get out of there. I had read how whales had tipped over the old whaling boats and killed the whalers. A flirt of the tail could crush *Number 9* like an egg. They could roll up beneath and flip it over. And what chance would I have in that water? I ran forward, was leaning over to haul in the anchor, when a dim shape rushed out of the depths. Involuntarily I jumped back. He surfaced not a hundred feet away, spouted, rolled broadside with head lifted. He seemed to look me over, then arched his back and went down. Maybe, I thought, if I remained still, I would be all right. Anyway, if I tried to run for it now I might pass over a whale as he came up. At least they knew where I was. I could hope that made me safer.

I remained on deck almost an hour watching them. They continued to play about, sometimes so close I felt the spray of their spouting, sometimes half a mile away. Finally I decided I was safe enough, so I returned to the galley where I cooked a rousing big meal.

Sleepy Bay seems a favorite hangout for whales during storms. It is quiet and deep, and there is a growth on bottom that they feed on. I have lain in there a number of times since, but never again during a storm, if I can avoid it.

Whenever I am tempted to think of these big fellows as just clumsy, playful brutes, I remember Paddy's experience or the whale that wrecked the Port Chalmers Trap.

One day a call came to rush to the Squire Island Trap. A whale had become entangled in the wire and was wrecking it.

Squire Island is in that part of the Sound where I had seen most whales, not far from Sleepy Bay. Another Paddy and the whale, I told myself.

It was a long ten-hour run from Cordova. I was still a half mile from the trap when I began passing chunks of blubber floating down the bay. As I drew near I saw the watchman on the logs. He had a butcher knife wired to a pole and was stabbing down into the water. Looking tired and hot he leaned on his makeshift spear as he watched me pull into the trap.

I called through the open window, "I hear you caught a whale."

He tossed a shock of long blond hair out of his eyes and said grimly, "You'll see, brother! You'll see!"

I jumped to the logs, took a turn about a cleat with the bow line and went forward to see. He was not more than six feet under water and was caught about the middle. He had punched halfway through the wire and the strain on the bulging mesh had pinched the hole shut; that and his high dorsal fin held him tight. I saw the raw, open wounds where the watchman had carved out slabs of blubber in an effort to reach a vital spot. I saw all thirty and more feet of black torpedo length. Even as I stared he arched fiercely upward, the ugly head broke surface and he blew almost in my face. I saw rows of teeth, two inches in diameter, the most terrible in the sea.

"It's the first killer whale I ever saw close up," the watchman was saying. "I pumped two boxes of .45-90 shells into him and I've been carving on him God knows how long. He has been in there eleven hours. How tough do they get?"

I had no answer. This was the first one I had seen close up, too, and I did not like what I saw.

The killer whale is the one creature I fear above all others. He is hated and feared by all sea life. He is a gangster, a vicious, senseless murderer, the wolf of the sea. Like the wolf he travels in packs of thirty or forty, charging across the sea attacking anything that lives. In packs they have been known to charge a fifty-foot boat and rip chunks of planking from the bottom.

A killer whale will trap a seal on an ice flow, dive beneath, tip the flow over and dump the hapless seal into his waiting jaws. He will attack and kill a fifteen-hundred-pound polar bear in the same manner.

He is also called Orca or blackfish. His length will exceed thirty feet. When his high dorsal fin knifes the water, the sea lions and seals rush for the beach. They will even face a man with a rifle in preference to taking to the sea while the killer whale is about. A sixty-ton whale has been known to become so paralyzed with fright at sight of the killer whale that he will lie helpless while the killer rips a banquet from his mountainous bulk, or worse still, forces open his mouth and eats his tongue.

The killer whale is the one animal I will shoot on sight. As many as I have shot I have yet to kill one. I have blown chunks of flesh the size of my fist out of them without even slowing them down.

During dives I have often seen half a sea lion, the carcass giving evidence of having been sliced in half by one snap of powerful jaws. I found a giant dead halibut with a single bite ripped from its middle. I believe this was the work of killer whales. No other sea monster's mouth is large enough to perform such feats.

When I see the high dorsal fin slicing the sea I sit safe and snug aboard the boat until I know he has left the neighborhood.

There is no telling how many holes that have been laid to other causes he has ripped in traps. This was the first time I had known of one to become caught.

The watchman's next words went right to my stomach. "Brother, I don't envy you the job of taking him out."

I thought about that. I would have to go into the sea to cut him loose. Once he was free what might happen? Would he head for sea or turn on me in his rage? I could not get out fast enough to avoid his lightning strike—and he could slice a thousand-pound sea lion in half with a single snap. Even if he took off, ignoring me, I stood a good chance of having my air line caught in his rush. And the way he strained intermittently at the wire he might not wait until I had finished the cutting job before he would rip free. I believed that once

I had cut him halfway loose he possessed the strength to tear out the remainder of the wire. There was but one man to tend air and telephone lines, the compressor, and to help me out of the sea in a hurry if need be.

I considered refusing to do the job. I argued with myself. "Why not call the cannery short wave and have them send out a tender with a charge of dynamite to kill the whale? No one would blame me for refusing to enter the water with this animal.

"It would take hours for a tender to arrive, and in the meantime the trap would do no fishing. It was my job to keep it fishing. But I had never agreed to take on a killer whale. And what difference did a few hours make?

"A few hours could mean the loss of a trapful of fish. The cannery would not like that. The story would get around and affect other jobs. It went even deeper. To back off once because of danger made it twice as easy the second time. Soon my courage and confidence would leak away and I would be another fair-weather diver. I would be through." It was this last that really decided me.

The watchman said, "They tell me these guys are awful dangerous. How are you going to do it?"

"I'll go down and cut him out."

"You can do that? For sure?" he asked, surprised.

"With a little luck, yes."

We tied the boat to the trap about twenty feet from the whale and I got into the suit. Twice during that time he heaved his head above water, blew fiercely and went down, to shake the trap with a fresh burst of tail lashing and body twisting.

When I was ready I sat a moment, considering a life line, then discarded it. No man could help me if I got tangled up with this fellow as he took off, or if he turned on me. I hoped to cut him loose and get out before he realized what had happened. In case he took off, I would try to keep my lines free, giving him a clear path to the sea. I asked the watchman if he had ever worked with a diver before.

"You're the first one I ever seen," he said.

I explained about the compressor, air pressure, how to put on the helmet and lock it. I told him how I meant to do the job. "I'll wait until he blows before I start. Then I'll go down, do the job, and get out before he blows again. I don't want him coming up and thrashing around while I'm in there and he is half cut out. I'll begin at the top on the opposite side about five feet from him. I'll cut a circle around him ending at the top on this side. Keep my air line tight when I'm on this side. I don't want any slack he can get tangled up in if he suddenly takes off. Soon as I finish I'll blow myself to the surface and get out."

"What if something goes wrong?" he asked. "Suppose he tackles you. What do I do?"

"If you can get hold of me, help me get out; but never yank on the air line, whatever you do. Well, let's get the helmet on."

Ready to dive, I climbed down the ladder into the water and clung to the trap wire about fifteen feet away from the whale. I waited for him to blow again. Being in the same water with an animal whose business is ripping off arms and legs made me terribly conscious of those parts of my anatomy. I imagined I could feel the blood pumping strongly through them and every nerve seemed raw. A minute later the whale's head came up, he blew, thrashed around a little and went down again.

I hit the chin valve, sank below him, then eased across the wire, hand over hand. I passed under him and went up the far side. I began cutting above him, working down. This was the most dangerous spot. The air line passed beneath him and if he ripped free before I cut across to the other side, he might take the air line with him when he left.

I clung to the wire with one hand and operated the cutters at top speed with the other.

The whale exploded into violent action once, whipping his tail about and throwing his ugly head from side to side. The trap shook. The wire stretched and strained. I clutched it with both hands and held my breath. In a moment he became quiet again and I resumed cutting feverishly, watching the cutters with one eye, the killer, but an arm's length away, with the other. The water was clear, too clear. This close, the teeth looked twice as large and ten times as dangerous.

I was down to the bottom of the cut. About three minutes had passed. I sliced across under him and started up the last side. Four minutes I told myself. He would be coming up in a couple more. He was half cut out now. When he moved again he would feel the slack the cut was making and all hell might break loose.

I did not realize how frantically I was working until I stabbed at the wire and missed. Then I felt the sweat streaking my face, felt the bone-dryness of my throat. I was panting as though I had been running hard. I forced myself to slow down, to get the rhythm of slide, snip, slide, snip again.

Then the tender's voice said, "It's about time he came up

for air, ain't it?" It startled me so that I almost dropped the
cutters.

I was four, five, six feet up on the third side. The wire
began to bulge outward. Soon the whale could not help but
feel the lessening strain. I was up a third of the way, a half.
My arm cried for rest. Cramps stiffened my fingers, crept
into my palm and wrist. I knew I was working slower. But
before the face plate the jaws of the cutters ate up the wire
with surprising speed. I was conscious of the shadow of
Number 9 near me. I saw light beams dancing on the surface
ten feet away. Ten feet from safety.

The killer whale was now held by little more than a quarter
of the mesh. He actually floated in the hole. I was facing in-
ward and I watched his tail for any sign that presaged another
try for freedom. At the first flicker of movement I was getting out—fast!

I was almost to the top of the cut—three-fourths finished.
Then it happened! There was no telltale twitch of tail or
movement of body to warn me. I felt, rather than saw, his
sudden burst of energy. The wire bulged, throwing me back
away from it, torn strands whipped past the face plate. They
dragged across the breastplate and helmet. I heard, or perhaps imagined I heard, the squeal of ripping wire. I grabbed
at the air valve to pour air into the suit, missed, and grabbed
again.

I shot to the surface, streaked hand over hand along the
wire, up the ladder into the boat.

My fears were groundless. The killer whale headed straight
out to sea, taking a ten-foot wire necklace with him.

I sat on deck and the watchman began unscrewing the

wing nuts of the breastplate. I was still shaking and that "all gone" feeling was an ache in my stomach.

"Why, that wasn't bad at all," the watchman said cheerfully. "We didn't have a thing to worry about. He took out of here like a scared rabbit. Say, how much do you get for this dive?"

"A hundred dollars," I said.

"No kidding? A hundred bucks for a lousy ten minutes work? Man, I sure am in the wrong business."

14

The Trap Watchmen

I have been surprised at the cool, efficient manner with which untried tenders have operated to get me out of trouble. It is a tough spot for a tender, the moment he realizes that beneath the sea a man is fighting for his life on the other end of the line he holds. That came home full force the day I dove the Woodcock Point Trap.

The watchmen, a pair of young fellows, were helping. Ed West was tall, lean and whipcord tough. Frank Noble was a wiry little fellow with thinning brown hair and big, serious blue eyes behind thick glasses.

As usual, when they had dismantled the trap the year before, the wire had been dropped to bottom. Normally the action of the sea eats it away during the winter. This time it had not. The bottom of the heart was a mess of loose, rotting coils almost fifteen feet high.

Sixty feet down I was threading my way through these miniature mountains when the *tunk-tunk* of the compressor stopped. On the heels of that Frank's voice said, "Virg, the compressor's down. The drive pulley broke."

"How much air in the tank?" I asked.

"The gauge says forty pounds."

Forty pounds! Ten minutes of air at most and I dared not surface where I was. I was sixty feet down and had traveled more than half the width of the heart. There was perhaps seventy feet of air line lying among these coils of wire. If I tried to surface here and a coil caught the air line before I reached the top I'd be trapped between bottom and surface and would have wasted half the remaining air in the ascent. The only sensible thing was to go back the way I had come and surface beside the boat. There was no time to spare. I told Frank to keep a tight air line and headed straight across the heart. The rolls of wire got bigger and thicker, instead of smaller as I had hoped. Soon it was a solid wadded-up mass before me.

Frank's voice said, "You got twenty pounds left. Better hurry!"

There was no time to go back now and look for a better way, and there was not enough air in the tank to inflate and float to the surface. The only out was to climb over this mess. I cut down the air to economize on what was left and almost immediately began breathing stale air.

I went up and over the first big roll, the second. I was halfway up the third when the buckles on my shoes caught in the wire. I tried to yank free. The rotting mesh broke and dropped me through to my knees. When I stopped Ed began yanking on the air line. I shouted, "I'm hung up. Don't pull until I tell you to."

I tried jerking first one leg then the other. Each time the weight of my body drove them deeper. Finally, I lay down, twisted about, got my hands down and began frantically to work the wire off my left leg. For the first time in my diving experience I was starving for air. It is a terrible, frightening sensation. I panted, open-mouthed, fighting to fill my lungs with air that was not there. Sweat poured down my face, running into my eyes, mouth and nose. Sickness was in my stomach and nausea filled my throat. The protective padding of air in the suit was trickling away. The crushing strength of the sea began to bend my ribs. Panic was suddenly in the helmet with me. I fought it as hard as I fought the wire, as hard as I fought to breathe. I had to work, had to concentrate on the things I was doing by touch alone.

Frank's voice said, sharp and frightened, "Virg, you loose yet? Can't we do something? Can't we help? You've only got ten pounds left. Ten pounds, Virg!"

"I'm tangled in the wire," I panted. "Just stand by." I got my left leg free and began on the right. I felt for the buckles, the wire, and twisted and yanked savagely. Wire ripped and tore. I felt it cut into my palms, felt the burn of salt water in torn flesh. Suddenly the foot was free.

"Virg, five pounds! You only got five pounds of air left. Are you loose yet? For God's sake, hurry!"

I slid off the roll of wire and panted, "Haul in!" and started across the trap again. I tried to force my way between the mountains of wire, and knew I would never make it. There was but one way out—over the top—and it had to be fast. My legs were shaking and that woozy feeling that precedes passing out was creeping over me.

I charged up, over and down, clawing frantically. How I got across without again snagging the buckles, without falling through the rotting mesh to my shoulders, I will never know. The next thing the air line rose straight up. The boat was sixty feet above.

I mumbled, "Haul me up! Haul up!" and grabbed the air line above the helmet so the weight would not pull on the fitting and rip it loose. I was whisked to the surface and the face plate jerked open. Ed and Frank bent over holding me on the ladder, still hip-deep in the sea, while I gulped air.

Frank's voice trembled and his eyes behind the glasses were enormous, "My God, Virg! That was close. That was awful close!"

"Close!" Ed's voice cracked. He pointed at the compressor gauge. "Hell, he was practically gone."

I looked past him at the gauge. The needle stood at empty.

Later Frank said, "What you need is one of those diving rigs you strap on your back, an aqualung. There'd be no compressor to break down and no lines to foul up."

He was partially right. I had considered the aqualung but had given it up for a number of reasons. First, an aqualung is good for only about sixty minutes' air supply if you are careful and conserve your air. If you are working hard it will last only thirty or forty. I work hard repairing a trap and sometimes I am under two or three hours. Second, the deep-water suit, as mine is called, has a constant padding of air about the diver's body which protects him from the freezing cold of these Northern seas. No aqualung diver could stand the frigid cold of this Northern water more than a few minutes. Third, my metal helmet is a fine protection against bumps. Every season I pound dents out of the helmet. And last, there is no means of communication between the aqualung diver and the surface. In repairing a fish trap, constant communication between the diver and his helpers on top is vitally important. There are many lines to be tightened and slacked, information to be sent to those on top, requests for tools and material to be sent the diver. The cumbersome and heavy deep-water outfit is the only practical one for diving a fish trap.

It was not long after the Woodcock Point incident that a storm landed on the mainland with terrific impact. At the height of its fury, it hurled the warehouse at Ellamar Cannery into the sea, where it sank beneath forty feet of water. The warehouse was packed with seven thousand cases of canned salmon valued in excess of a hundred thousand dollars. The storm lasted a day and a night. The morning after, I was there and ready to dive. I knew that salvaging this pack called for speed. The sea would eat through the thin tin in a few days and ruin the fish.

Ellamar sits on the bank of a beautiful, and usually well-protected bay. The cannery is a cluster of white buildings against the green of Ellamar Mountain. Ellamar was formerly a rich copper mine that had played out. Many of the mine buildings are being used by the cannery. A theatre with fine wooden columns has been turned into a men's dormitory. The cannery store is in one of the old mining store buildings. Rusting mining machinery litters the place. An old tailing pile, the dirt and rock from which the copper had been sifted, is visible on the beach.

It was a fine post-storm day. The sky was rain-washed and clear; the sun was a brilliant ball. We pulled into the bay and tied to a stub of piling above the spot where the warehouse had sunk. We had two boats for the job. The diving equipment was set up on one; the other towed two scows, onto which we were to load the salmon cases for transfer back to the cannery. There they would be checked for damage and recooked.

The tide was out. Broken timbers and pieces of plank floated about. Down through the gray, silty water I could barely make out the shape of the warehouse roof. I knew it would be tricky and dangerous down there. There was a forest of jagged-ended broken timbers, planks studded with rows of nails and bolts, razor-sharp torn metal edges, and pointed ends of broken pipe—everything to rip the diving suit. To make matters worse, the inside of that building would be in deep gloom. Luckily I had a second suit, an old patched relic I had been wearing in the traps while I saved the new one.

My two helpers had never worked a diver before. I wished I had a pair of experienced men—just in case. My helpers were Roy and Elmer Barker, owners of the tender I was diving from, the *North King*.

I went through the business of explaining the diving procedure. I thought I covered everything, but I left out one of the most important details.

Then I got into the patched suit, stepped off into the sea and sank to the roof of the warehouse. I ripped a hole in the roof large enough to take out the jitneys—the small four-wheeled machines used for pulling loads about the cannery. Through this hole we would also lower slings to take out the salmon cases. I did not want my air and telephone lines going down through the same opening out which slings and jitneys would come so I stepped off the roof, went to bottom and under the back of the building where it tilted some

fifteen feet off bottom. I found a row of jagged holes in the
floor and floated through one into the building.

The building lay in twilight gloom. Broken, nail-studded
timbers and planks made shadowy patterns about me. A
mountain of salmon cases had skidded to the low side of the
building. The hole I had ripped in the roof hung a pale light
column into the grayness. Waiting for me in the middle of
the hole swung a hook and cable from the boat on the surface. I floated up and reached for the hook. The next instant
I was plummeting downward.

I snatched at the air valve and poured air into the suit.
Nothing happened. Then I felt the cold rush of water. Somehow I had ripped the suit and the sea was pouring in. The
ragged ends of floor timbers flashed past the face plate, then
open sea. I struck bottom hard and fell full length. Water
gushed into the helmet, filling it. I scrambled upright and
the inpouring air drove the water down to my chin where
it stopped, an inch or two below my mouth, held there by
the flow of air into the helmet.

I felt the looseness at my right cuff and held it up before
the face plate. The full length of the cuff was ripped. In
reaching for the cable I had snagged it on a broken strand
of the cable. The cuff, being pure rubber, is the easiest part of
the suit to rip. I had to get out of here now!

Then I discovered I had fallen through a different hole
from the one I had first entered. The air line now went up
inside the warehouse through one hole, across the floor and
down another to me. I said into the telephone, "I've ripped
the suit and I'm coming up. I will have to climb the air line
about fifteen feet and go down through another hole before
you can pull me up. So take a good grip on that line." There

was no answer. I yelled, "Roy, you hear me?" The telephone was dead. Of course, the connections in the helmet were soaked with sea water now. They could not know what had happened to me down here.

I took hold of the air line and pulled experimentally. There was enough loose line going through other holes and around corners to take my weight. I began climbing toward the warehouse floor. Climbing a rope in a gym suit is tough but doing the trick on sea bottom with a diving suit full of water is twice as hard. I made the floor, went through, crossed to the other hole out which the air line ran and jumped through. Again I went flat when I landed, and again water poured into the helmet and stayed until I scrambled upright and the air pressure drove it back. A half-dozen steps and I was out from under the warehouse. The air line rose straight up.

I yanked on the line as a signal to haul me up. I yanked again and again. Nothing happened. They held the line tight but refused to pull. My yanking, I guessed, told them something was wrong but never having worked a diver they were simply holding on, the one thing they knew for sure to do. They were trusting to me to make the necessary moves since all the line shaking indicated I was very much alive. I began climbing again.

Finally the bottom of the boat took shadowy shape. A few more feet and I could see it clearly with Roy and Elmer's faces staring down at me. I motioned toward the diving ladder. They swung me that way and hauled up until I gripped the bottom rungs and climbed aboard.

A minute later I was on deck and they were stripping off the suit. "We knew something must be wrong the way the air line kept shaking but we couldn't figure what," Elmer said. "We decided the best thing was to hang tough and let you do what you wanted. We knew if there was any danger you would tell us. That ripping the suit and getting the phone wet is a funny one. I guess this diving's not so simple."

I took time out to change clothes and to have a cup of coffee. Then I got into the new diving suit and this time explained, "If I jiggle the air line four times, pull until something gives." When I went down again I ripped another hole in the roof about twenty feet from the first and went in through the top.

The jitneys were the first things removed. Then the sling was lowered through the hole and I began filling it with salmon cases. As each scow was loaded it was taken to the cannery. There the cans were thoroughly washed, inspected for rust spots and damage, then returned to the pressure cooker and recooked. As a final precaution every can was lacquered to ensure a tight seal.

A case of salmon weighs about fifty pounds. Under forty feet of water, that weight was cut to three or four. I could toss those cases about as easily as a basketball. I could sail a case into the sling with either hand from as far away as I could see.

Strange as it may seem, you can actually become so interested in what you are doing under water that you completely forget where you are. For a time I enjoyed practicing one-handed shots. Those cases would arch gracefully through the murk and settle into the sling. I began close up and worked back, making perfect bull's-eyes with every throw until I reached the limit of my vision. That was not far. But with the natural distortion of the water it gave the impression of shooting half the length of a basketball court.

Suddenly I felt the water climbing around my legs again. I had snagged the new suit. I said, "I'm coming up! Got a rip in the suit again," and headed for the hole in the roof. There was still enough air in the suit to float me slowly upward.

The hole was a small rip in the leg, probably from a nail. I patched it and went down again. I quit playing star forward and tended to business. But no matter how carefully I worked, or which way I turned, I was surrounded by things sharp and cutting. I ripped the suit twice more that day. One was a long cut, and again the water got into the helmet. I got out on the roof and the boys pulled me up. But we made good progress and scow loads of salmon were heading for the cannery at regular intervals.

By the end of the second day we had removed about a third of the pack and the new diving suit was beginning to look like a well-patched old inner tube. At the rate it was ripping I would be lucky if it lasted out the job.

At the end of the third day we had removed a good half of the pack but there was still a mountain of cases below.

It was the fourth day late in the afternoon and I was busily tossing cases into the sling when Elmer yelled, "Virg, the warehouse is breaking loose! Get out, quick!" That instant the floor heaved upward, sending the salmon case flying from my hands and knocking me flat. Cases of salmon shot out of the gloom around me. A six-by-six timber slammed down before the face plate, dragging the jagged half of a plank filled with spikes. I climbed to my feet, expecting every moment to be swatted by a timber or a case of flying salmon.

I started for the hole in the roof at that heartbreakingly slow-motion underwater walk. The floor twisted and heaved and threw me flat again. I began crawling on all fours, clawing aside salmon cases, dragging myself under nail- and sliver-studded timbers and planking.

I realized what had happened and should have prepared for it. The salmon we had taken out had lightened the warehouse. It suddenly righted itself and was floating down the bay on the out-running tide. I remembered that the boat was tied to the piling stub. If I did not get out quickly the floating warehouse would take up the slack of my air line, rip it from the suit and I would be stranded here.

The air line tightened, yanked me forward skidding across the floor to bring up tight against the mountain of cases. "There goes the slack!" I thought, and tried to scramble over the pile. The stretching air line held me pinned down against the cases. I was helpless. In a couple of seconds the air line would snap from the helmet.

Then the pressure was gone. I scrambled up thinking, "This is it! The air line is gone!" Then I saw it stretched out ahead of me, disappearing through the hole in the roof. I heard the *tunk-tunk* of the compressor and felt air circulating through the helmet. I did not question the why of this miracle. I scrambled over the remaining cases and went up through the hole in the roof in a headlong dive.

The moment the tenders hauled me aboard I saw why I was alive. In some fast thinking they had cut the boat loose from the piling stub. She was floating calmly down the bay beside the warehouse.

Strange as it seems, few people remember the near-tragic incidents such as the warehouse job. They never forget the

humorous ones. An incident many like to remind me of oc-
curred at Bligh Island.

I had gone to inspect the trap for holes after a whale had
nudged the wire. The watchmen were a pair of happy-go-
lucky young fellows.

I was in the heart, some seventy feet down, when I smelled
smoke. For a moment I thought something was burning on
deck and it was coming through the compressor. A wisp of
smoke drifted into the helmet and curled before the face
plate. Then I felt the heat against my hip pocket. I had forgotten to take the matches out of my pocket. My movements
and the pressure at seventy feet had created a friction that
had lit them.

I yelled, "I'm on fire! I'm coming up. Get a bucket of
water!"

"Man, you're crazy," the telephone tender laughed.
"You're on the bottom of the ocean."

Not any more. I was shooting toward the surface as fast
as air would take me, and my pistol pocket was really frying.
When I broke the surface, the helmet was a swirl of smoke
that almost blinded me.

They yanked me up the ladder, twisted off the helmet and
dumped water down my back while they laughed like mani-
acs. "Nobody will ever believe this!" they howled. "Nobody! You should have seen your face, Virg. You should
have seen it!"

15

Marooned off Valdez

In Alaska, I long ago discovered, the unusual is taken for granted. The attitude seems to be, "If you hang around here long enough, something out of the ordinary will happen to you. Because it does, is no reason for us to become excited."

A good example was the pirating trip I made in Nick Holland's *Pelican*. Nick was a big, good-natured Alaskan with a two week's growth of whiskers and a broken nose. He was a fish pirate, and a good one. This day he was short a crew member and asked me to go. Diving was at a standstill. I had completed the preseason inspection dives and was now waiting for call-backs. The season had just opened and the salmon run had not yet hit. I agreed to make one trip with Nick and his crewman Cal Roberts.

Next day we were off across the sea searching for traps filled with fish to rob. We looked into every trap on the Sound and found no salmon. The days were twenty hours long and bright and hot. The thermometer stood at ninety-two degrees, breaking a heat record of long standing.

The morning of the fifth day we ran out of grub. On a small boat you carry just enough so you can clean it up while it is still fresh, then put into port and restock. We planned to restock in Valdez.

During that morning I took a drink from the water barrel. The barrel had stood on deck in the beating sun five days. The water tasted like it and I said so.

"Dump it," Nick said. "We can refill in Valdez."

I upended the barrel and that precious water spilled into the sea.

A little later we raised a steamer. She was standing several miles off Columbia Glacier to give a load of bug-eyed tourists a look at the world's largest active glacier. From Columbia she would follow the tourist route into Valdez.

We had barely left the steamer astern when a shark rose dead ahead and cruised toward us, his dorsal fin slicing the water. Nick, who hated sharks, snatched the pistol from the shelf and rushed outside for a shot.

I heard the shot but saw no water spout or indication the shark had been hit. I glanced back and saw Nick sitting on the deck holding his right arm. A red stain was spreading across the sleeve. The gun lay against the rail. He had tripped and fallen going out the wheelhouse. The gun had flown from his hand, struck the rail and fired; the bullet had entered his arm.

We got him inside, examined the wound and bandaged it with strips from a torn towel. The bullet had entered several inches below the elbow. It had shattered the bone and emerged through a ragged, bloody hole. Nick needed a doctor.

Cal took the wheel and we raced down the Narrows toward

Valdez at full throttle. We were within sight of the town when it happened. One moment we were churning down the narrowest part of the channel, the next the *Pelican* was heeling to starboard, running wild. Cal spun the wheel but she kept swinging and rocked back through her own wake in an explosion of spray and engine roar.

He cut the motor and looked at Nick.

"Steering cable has come loose," Nick said.

I went below and traced the length of both cables. They were tight in their blocks. I reported this and Nick said soberly, "Then we've dropped the rudder. It happened once before when the pin sheared off. This is bad."

At the moment it was bad only in that it would hold us up a day to fix the rudder and make Nick a little late in getting to a doctor. It would have been impossible to foresee more. We lay in a calm sea, the day was bright and cloudless. We were in plain sight of a town of more than fifteen hundred persons less than three miles off, an easy distance to spot a boat in distress. A steamer was due. She could drop a line aboard and tow us in. Any moment a boat would put out from town or come over the horizon. Our wait must be short.

An hour dragged by. No boat came over the horizon or put out from Valdez. No steamer came. A bush pilot rose out of the town and streaked up the Narrows, passing low over us in a battered yellow float plane. We waved and yelled. The pilot waved out the window.

Nick held his wounded arm and scowled at the retreating plane, then around at the empty sea. "Sure hope somebody comes soon," he muttered.

"A boat will come," Cal said. "One has just got to. This is the only waterway into Valdez."

The sun started its long swing down the sky. We became thirsty and hungry, but neither of these was bad. What we needed was a boat to tow us in or a short-wave radio to call out help. We had no radio and no boat came.

The bleeding stopped in Nick's arm and the numbness began to wear off. He paced the deck mumbling angrily, "A thousand seiners in the Sound but none here. Where in hell are they all?"

The sun finally dipped into the sea and the Northern night was upon us. Then the treacherous fog, that is so much a part of Alaska's coastal weather, rolled down off the high peaks and over us so thick I could not see the bow fifteen feet off. The steamer that at any time would come down the channel took on fearful meaning. We had no fog horn, no whistle and our lights would do no good.

We sat on deck, talked in low voices and waited for the first sound to break the silence, for the sight of a towering steel bow rushing out of the fog upon us.

"If they sink us, they can stop and pick us up," Cal said.

"In this fog they'll never know they ran us down," Nick answered. "If they did it would take half a mile to stop or get a boat over. They would be too far away to find three men swimming in this soup, too long getting to us. Ten minutes is about our limit in these waters." Nick sat on the rail, bent over holding his bullet-shattered arm with his left hand. I could see the dark stain that had oozed through the bandage on his forearm.

I could visualize how it would happen, the steel bow slicing into us, hurling us into the frigid Alaskan sea. There would be a few frantic strokes, a cry or two lost in the fog and night, then the black depths of Valdez Narrows would drag us down.

"If the steamer crashes us," Nick said, "look for a piece of wreckage to cling to and yell at the top of your lungs. There's not one chance in a thousand it will help. But it's the only thing we can do."

So we sat, and waited, and listened, and the short night hours passed, yet it seemed the longest night of my life.

Dawn burned the fog away and once again the sea stretched about us bright, calm and empty. Again Valdez mocked us in the near distance. The day turned sickeningly hot and the sun volleyed off the water. Hunger was an ache in our stomachs, but it was thirst that really bothered us. To make it worse, over on shore, so close I almost seemed to hear its rushing, a stream foamed down the mountain from a high-up glacier. It would be cold, clear and wonderfully wet.

Yesterday's battered yellow plane rushed down the Narrows toward town. We waved and yelled again with no success.

Nick's elbow had become stiff during the night, the flesh red and swollen. His face, beneath the whiskers, was pinched and gray. He looked at the stream tumbling down the mountain, unconsciously wet his lips, then deliberately sat down with his back to it. He finally said out of a silence, "I once helped bring a guy out of the mountains who had shot himself through the foot. The Doc had to take it off." He rubbed his arm gently. "How long does it take for gangrene to set in?"

"That's no way to talk," I said. "We're going to get out of here."

"Sure. But when?"

"Soon as a boat shows and that could be any minute. You know that."

"We said that yesterday."

"I been thinking," Cal said. "If we fastened the hatch cover to a rope and dragged it astern on the port side, maybe it would create enough drag to offset the swing to starboard."

We got out a rope, tied it to the hatch and tossed the hatch overboard. Cal started the motor while Nick and I watched. The *Pelican* cut around in the same sharp circle with the hatch riding on the surface like a surfboard.

The hatch needed weight to hold it under. We dragged the anchor aft and lashed it to the hatch and tried again. It was no good. The moment the speed increased the hatch rose and skipped along the surface.

Nick said, "Maybe I could lay on the hatch and paddle ashore."

"It would sink and you've got only one arm to paddle with," I pointed out. "Besides it would take an hour and no one can live that long in this water. If there was a chance I'd go."

He rubbed his shattered arm and mumbled, "Okay! Okay! But I'm not going to take this forever, not when there's a town this close. I'll do something." He turned away, lifted the lid of the water barrel from force of habit, dropped it and went forward. He was big and tough but that toughness was being chipped away by the constant pain.

Cal asked, "How long does gangrene take, Virg?"

"I don't know," I said. "Not long enough."

Later the battered yellow plane went over again, outbound. We shouted and waved and Nick held his bloody arm aloft for the pilot to see. For a reason I will never understand he found nothing unusual in our lying so long in one spot. Nick cursed him out of sight with a savagery that made me fear for the pilot's life if they ever met.

The plane was our only break in the eternally empty, glaring day.

We took turns trying to sleep. But empty bellies, cotton-dry throats and nagging worry left Cal and me rolling in the bunks until we gave up and returned to the hopeless vigil. Nick would not lie down, he scarcely sat more than a minute. He paced the deck and wheelhouse hour after hour.

We argued the reasons for no help. The boats from Valdez must all be on the seining grounds. Out there the run must have hit and the boys were raking them in so fast there was no time to make a town. Maybe they had changed the schedule on the cruise ship and she was bypassing Valdez this trip.

Night finally came, its coolness bringing a measure of relief from thirst but none from hunger. Again the fog rolled thickly over us. This time I welcomed it, even if it meant the liner would cut us in two.

The liner did not come. The night hours dragged slowly by again.

Dawn lifted the fog and we anxiously scanned the horizon. I knew instantly this day was going to be different. Valdez still squatted on the mud flats three miles off and the sea was bright, calm and empty. The difference was the belt of black clouds, like thundercaps, ringing the horizon; the vacuum-like hush that lay like a pall over the sea. No inquisitive seal poked his head up to stare at us, no gull's cry broke the stillness. All life in and out of the sea seemed to have run for safety. It was as if the world waited on tiptoe for some terrible thing to happen.

For a moment no one spoke, then Cal said in a worried voice, "I don't like the looks of that."

"A williwaw!" Nick said. "I'd bet my life it will be a williwaw. We won't have a prayer if we're caught out here."

Williwaw! The word was a block of ice in my stomach. Williwaw is an Indian word for the big wind peculiar to the Alaskan coast. It roars across the sea with velocities often above a hundred miles an hour, piling up giant waves, wrecking shore installations. It will snap the inch-thick steel cables holding floating traps and toss the traps onto the beach, a mass of twisted wire and broken logs. Ten-thousand-ton liners and seiners scurry for the protection of ports, the lee of islands or protected bays. The williwaw-wrecked skeletons of dozens of ships and hundreds of fish boats litter the floor of the sea or lie rotting, rusting shells, along this rock-bound coast.

I knew how it would come. The clouds would spread across the sky darkening the day, turning the sea lead gray. Then the hurricanelike wind would hit. We would not last ten minutes.

"How long before it will hit?" I asked.

Nick studied the sky. With this new danger he had momentarily forgotten his shattered arm. "Three—maybe four hours. But we can't wait any longer. We've got to get someplace quick."

"If we could only fix that hatch up like a rudder," Cal said.

"Impossible," I said. But it had started a train of thought. I looked at the deck and the cabin bulkhead. "If we had a plank we could make a sweep over the stern like they did on Mississippi River barges a hundred years ago."

"A sweep?" Nick said. "You mean like a big oar? Say! there used to be a pair of oars down below, up forward of the engine."

I dived into the engine room, rummaged through the black hole forward and found them beneath a tangle of old rope.

From the top of the turntable that jutted over the stern they barely touched the water.

"Try them over the side," Nick advised.

The side was low enough to put two feet of oar in the water and leave enough oar over for a good handhold to brace against the forward surge of the boat. But we had lost our rudder effect.

As if he expected it to work Cal asked Nick, "Which way do you want to go and how will we work this?"

"You two will have to handle the oars. I'll stay inside where I can shut her off or throw her in reverse if anything happens," Nick said. He studied the channel into Valdez. "Awful narrow and she is going to be hard to steer. If we run aground I'll lose her sure. We could probably get ashore but it would take all day to hike to Valdez." He looked toward the open sea. "We're pointing that way and outside there will be plenty of steerage room. Twenty miles off there the *Ellen K* is lying in Galena Bay holding a fish barge. She's got a radio and can call out a plane. If we can make her, an hour later I can be to a doc. She can tow the *Pelican* to the cannery when she goes in. But we will be racing the storm across open water. If we don't beat it we're goners." He scrubbed a hand across his face uncertainly. "What do you boys want to do?"

"You're the skipper," Cal pointed out. "It's your boat and your arm."

Nick studied the sky again, then he said quietly, "All right, let's go!" and swung about and entered the wheelhouse.

We set our oars in the water, braced against the expected pull, and waited. The thought came, "This could be the mistake to end all mistakes." Then the motor started, we began to move. Pressure wrenched against the blades and it took all our strength to hold them in the water. The bow began the same swing to starboard. Then it slowed, stopped. Inch by inch it crept back on a straight course. We were heading out to sea, our destination a small protected bay where there was food, water and help for Nick's arm.

The *Pelican* kicked up a fine wake and the oar put constant pressure against me. My arms and shoulders began to ache. I lifted the oar for a moment's rest and the bow began to swing. I thrust it back and the pain came again. Sweat poured out of me. I was surprised there could be so much when my throat was so dry.

Cal glanced back, his face sweat-streaked, and shook his head.

Nick kept a sharp lookout for rocks and warned us a mile in advance. By digging deeper with the oars and holding with all our strength we were able to swing the bow a degree at a time and skin by.

But the storm was bearing down with startling speed. The cloud bank now darkened the sky. The sea was leaden, sullen, and possessed of a restlessness that made itself felt through the deck. Astern the land fell into the sea. There was no sight of land ahead.

Nick stepped on deck, studied the sky and sea and looking

over the side estimated our speed. Uncertainty was in his
look. He glanced at me, seemed about to say something, then
turned and re-entered the wheelhouse.

Wind hit us then. It began as a breeze and mounted with
a steady velocity you could feel. In minutes it had turned
the sea into whitecaps. The *Pelican* began to pitch. The whipping changed the pressure on the oar and snapped me about.
Sweat ran into my eyes, my open, panting mouth. My arms
and shoulders were weighted with lead.

Dead ahead a shore line rose out of the sea. Nick ducked
below to coax one more revolution out of the motor. It was
going to be that close. Overhead the sky was tumbling and
black. The *Pelican* rolled into a trough, throwing me outward. For one awful moment I hung there, looking down
into the smooth race of the trough flecked with foam, the
clear blue depths reaching down and down. I caught the
edge of the turntable, still holding tight to my oar with one
hand. The boat rolled to port, I pulled and fell back inside.

We were off course again. I drove the oar in and braced
but I knew we would never make it this time. I was too tired.
I knew Cal must be tired too, and the sea was too rough.
The wind hit us broadside and shoved us farther off course.
In a minute the full weight of the wind would smash us and
they could pick up the wreckage on shore after the storm.
This run across the sea had been a mistake.

Nick jumped out the wheelhouse door and threw his
weight, bad arm and all, against Cal's oar. That made the difference. The *Pelican* held her own against driving wind and
seas, then slowly crept back on course. We held her there
minute by minute while the land grew larger. The mouth of
the bay opened before us. It was Galena Bay.

We were literally blown in from the open sea, past a foaming point, into quiet water.

Cal turned and laughed then. "Man!" he said, "we never had it so good."

We found the *Ellen K* and her fish barge anchored at the far end of the bay. Captain Pete Lund caught our line and only nodded when we explained we had lost our rudder. "Figured so," he said. "Another ten minutes and you boys would never have made it."

While the *Ellen K*'s cook made lunch for us, Pete got on the radio. He raised Cordova almost immediately and ordered out a plane to pick up Nick.

A half hour later the float plane dropped out of the stormy sky and skimmed across the water toward us. It was the battered yellow job we had been waving at the past two days.

I glanced at Nick remembering how he had cursed the pilot. Gone was his anger now. He was staring like a man watching a lovely vision.

16

Fannie the Hike

Practically everyone who goes North is possessed with the dream of getting on a creek with a gold pan and trying his luck. After all, Alaska is the land of fabulous strikes.

Prospecting is a fever that gets into your blood like gambling. The gambler hopes to rake in the pot on the turn of a card. The prospector hopes to strike it rich with every shovelful of gravel.

I saw many watchmen, boatmen, seiners and cannery workers trying their luck along streams and bars during their spare hours. Their luck was slim. Usually the few precious grains they proudly hoarded in an aspirin bottle could have been bought in a curio shop for less than five dollars.

But I was determined to try my luck, too.

Mine would be no halfhearted amateur's attempt, thanks to the years I had mined Idaho's Salmon River Country as a kid. I questioned sourdoughs, bartenders, any old-timer I could corner. The sum of this accumulated knowledge added up to one likely territory, the Kantishna District on

228

the northwest side of Mt. McKinley National Park. The
Kantishna strike had been one of the last big ones and prospectors were still taking out a surprising amount of gold.

So it was that during the slack season I returned *Number 9*
to the cannery, stored the diving suit in the loft and took
off. It was late in the season to start, and as I was cramped for
time, I hired a bush pilot to fly me in and drop me off on a
gravel bar. Two days later I was in the Kantishna, and pack
on back, was hiking down Friday Creek.

The Kantishna is a rough land of timbered mountains and
valleys cut by rushing streams. Towering over this, dominat-
ing earth and sky, rose the chill, lordly cone of Mt. McKinley. *Denali,* or "Home of the Sun," the Indians call it.

This man-killing, sky-scraping scenery was surprisingly
like the Salmon River Country of Idaho. For a little, home-
sickness lay like a brick in my stomach.

I was tramping down Friday Creek, a brawling little stream
that popped in and out of brush patches and around rocks,
when I came upon a small, weather-blackened log cabin
perched on a bench some hundred feet above the creek. A
lazy rope of smoke trailed into the clear sky. A half-dozen
panting sled dogs sat spaced before the cabin, each on his
own chain, each with his own house. A trail wound up the
bench from the creek.

I was halfway up the trail when a woman's harsh voice
said, "You dirty so-and-so! get the hell out of here and stay
out."

I stepped through the line of dogs, who had set up a bed-
lam of barking at my approach, and into the open doorway.
A woman sat at a sawed plank table drinking milky liquid
from a tin cup. On the table before her were a bucket of

water and a jug. The jug's label read, *Grain Alcohol*. She tipped up her head and said in a harsh, blunt voice, "Hello, Jack! Pull up a chair and have a drink."

I had heard amazing stories of this woman. The old-timers had practically ordered me to stop there if I was in the neighborhood. Her name was Fannie Quigley, but to thousands of old Alaskan sourdoughs she was affectionately known as Fannie the Hike. She had acquired the name when, as a young woman in Alaska, she had hiked from strike to strike.

Fannie was born in a small Bohemian settlement in Nebraska. She possessed no formal education, could not even speak English until she was grown. But she had a sharp, inquisitive mind and had done an exceptional job of self-education. She could hold her own with most of the people who stopped by her cabin.

Nebraska's plains and small, snug towns held no allure for Fannie. When the big rush North came in '98, Fannie, then twenty-seven, packed a bag and hopped a boat heading for the Klondike with thousands of prospectors.

It was said Fannie could smell a strike coming. She would arrive by boat, dog sled or any other means of transportation. She brought along the tools of her trade—a Yukon stove, a tent, and a supply of staple foods such as flour, bacon and beans. She would pitch her tent in a likely spot, hang out a hand painted sign, MEALS FOR SALE, and go to work. When a strike died or a bigger one came along she struck her tent and was gone.

For years she operated a series of eating and boarding houses. Then in 1906 she went on her last stampede here in the Kantishna, married Joe Quigley, one of the strike dis-

coverers, and settled down. Her fame had spread through all
the North. She was a dog musher, prospector, trapper, hunter,
gardener, and one of the finest cooks in the territory. Had
I not heard so much about her, and already met other strange
and solitary characters of Alaska, this sight of her would have
amazed me.

She was close to seventy that day I met her, a short, slight
woman who weighed barely a hundred pounds. Her skin was
wrinkled and weather-burned. The wisps of hair escaping
from a man's battered felt hat were gray. She wore shoe pacs,
khaki choke-bore pants and a checkered wool shirt.

Now she poured an inch of alcohol into another cup, added
water, turning it milky, and shoved it toward me, "Drink
up, Jack," she said gruffly. "What brings you here?"

"I figured to do a little prospecting." I nudged the cup
aside.

"What's the matter," she scowled, "don't you like my
drink?"

"I don't think I can take it." I nodded toward the coffeepot bubbling on the back of the stove, "I sure would like a
cup of that, though."

She poured my drink into her cup and filled mine with
coffee. She brought out a loaf of homemade bread, a huge
cold roast of caribou and a wedge of blueberry pie. I pro-
tested that the coffee was plenty.

"Never saw a prospecting bum that wasn't starved," she
snapped. "You eat that."

I ate while she drank and talked. She had been talking to
herself when I came, not unusual for people much alone.
Now, with someone to listen, she rambled on about mining
in the Kantishna. The words tumbled out as she satisfied her

hunger for talk. "So you're going to prospect Friday Creek. I got three claims on it and they're no good. Friday Creek is not what it used to be, Jack. Take my advice, stay off it."

"I was told it was pretty good," I said.

"Not any more, Jack." She took a sip from the cup and pointed out the window. "See that, up on the hill?" Against the skyline was the crude shape of a cross, and the logs of a tent frame rose stark and dreary. "That guy starved to death trying to mine this creek."

"With you this close?" I chided. I knew her reputation for feeding everyone that came by. All she demanded, and got, was that you leave nothing on the plate, because she had to freight her year's grub a hundred miles by dog team during March. "You eat it all," I had been told she would warn a picky eater, "or you get the same plate next meal with the grub still on it."

Fannie grunted. "He had a weak stomach; couldn't eat my cooking."

She rambled on, talking about Eureka, the town a couple of miles away where two thousand miners used to live. Now it was a ghost town inhabited by one man, her good friend, Johnny Busia. That is what had happened to mining here. I listened and ate and stole glances about the room. The kitchen was small, most of one side was taken up by the plank table at which we sat. In a corner across the room there was a small porcelain sink with a drain through the plank floor. Gold pans sat about the walls, half-full of ore samples. A Yukon stove crouched against a far wall, throwing out a blaze of heat on this warm day. One wall was lined with plank shelves, the shelves loaded with ore samples and rocks. A half-dozen rusty pick heads were stacked in a corner with a small anvil and hammer.

She finished her drink and mine, and mixed herself another. She was not drunk, far from it. But her tongue had been loosened. The price of this meal, I decided, would be to listen, so I made myself a second sandwich and re-filled my coffee cup. Outside, the dogs quarreled and rattled their chains. The heat from the stove gradually died down.

Finally I said, "I had better get moving, if I expect to locate a place."

The moment I lifted my pack she spotted the pick. She yanked it loose and shoved it accusingly under my nose. "How do you expect to work with tools like that?" she demanded.

Before I could explain that it was on old one I had picked up for just this trip, she turned and shoved the blunt end into the open front of the stove and shook up the fire. When the metal finally turned red she carried the pick to the anvil and hammered the end expertly to a sharp point. "There—" she handed it back— "at least you got one thing right now."

Outside I noticed her garden for the first time. It was small, built in neat terraces bordered with rocks. There were rhubarb, potatoes, radishes, lettuce, beets, celery and turnips. They all looked luscious and thriving. There was not a weed in sight. This garden had been cared for with loving hands and planted by someone with a very green thumb. I said, "That's a fine garden. How do you get things to grow like that up here?"

"Ain't it a dandy?" For the first time her small, thin face broke into a smile. "You notice that soil is different from the rest on the bench? This bench soil's no good so I bring my garden soil up from Moose Creek by dog team. If I need more during the summer I pack it up on my back. Those rocks I carried up too. They're for a special reason. The sun heats the rocks and at night they hold the heat and keep the soil warm so things will grow then, too. We only got ten weeks growing season. I've got to make the most of it. When my husband, Joe, was alive this garden gave us enough for ourselves and company, too."

I thought of this frail little old woman carrying a sack of soil up from the creek on her back and said, "That's a lot of work for a few vegetables."

"Everything I grow or kill for food helps lighten the freight load," she answered promptly.

As I was leaving she asked suddenly, "You still going to scrabble around on Friday Creek?"

"Sure."

She glared at me. "You young bucks are all alike; all muscle and no brains—won't listen to anybody. I been here more years than you are old, and I'm telling you, you'll starve." She punched stringy gray hair back under the hat with angry fingers. "Go ahead and starve." She turned back into the cabin, then threw over her shoulder, "When you get hungry come down. I might as well feed you as bury you like I did that other one."

I went on up the creek stopping at each likely-looking bar and riffle, to run samples through my gold pan. This took time and my progress was slow. The second day after I left Fannie Quigley's I found good traces in a gravel bar along the creek bank. I took a number of samples, spending the day there. It was worth working, I decided, if I had a sluice box. A sluice box meant planks, and where would I find planks in this wilderness? Then I remembered Fannie's starvation claim on the hill above the cabin.

At my approach the dogs set up a chain-rattling, ear-splitting din. Fannie met me in the doorway. She wore the same shirt, hat and pants. "I knew it," she said in that rough voice, "starved out already."

"Have you any old planks I can use for a sluice box?" I asked.

"You found color in this Godforsaken creek?"

"I think so."

"You know color when you see it?" she demanded bluntly.

"I knew back in Idaho."

"Humph!" She studied me with bright old eyes, "Maybe you're like the Swede we had in Dawson. He wanted to know where to dig and for a joke the boys told him to go up on top of the mountain. He did, and struck one of the richest claims in the territory. But that was forty years ago and this ain't Dawson. Sure! You can have that lumber from the starvation claim, but come on in, dinner's almost ready."

It was the kind of meal you might expect in a first-class restaurant. There was moose steak, fresh blueberry pie with a feather-light crust, hot buns, vegetables from the garden, baked potatoes and cranberry jam.

I thought of her living here in the utter solitude of Mt. McKinley's immense shadow. One small, slight, gray-haired woman holding her own against this raw, brutal land. Except for an occasional passer-by her only company was the dogs. Her protection was her knowledge of the North, and the rifle that stood in the corner. Her strength seemed more an ironclad stubbornness of will than any physical attribute. Yet she carried soil up here from the creek on her back. It was nothing for her to spend a week out on her trap lines during the most savage winter weather.

I asked, "Don't you ever get lonesome or feel you are missing something, living way out here this way?"

"Guess I'm different from most women," she said. "The things they would miss aren't important to me. I'd be lost in a house on a city lot. I've got to have all outdoors to roam in. That's living. Sure, I work hard, but I love it. Those women in their shiny little houses in the city, work just as hard at housework. And most of them hate the monotony of it. There's no monotony on the trail. In all the years I have lived here I can find something different every day. So I've got the best of that deal." She glanced out the window at the rolling Kantishna hills. Her eyes were squinted against the strike of bright sunlight and her gruff voice was unusually gentle. "The first time I saw the Kantishna I knew this was where I belonged. I'll die here, Jack. There's not a hill out there I haven't left my boot prints on, and the loads of meat I've carried on my back over them would make an awful pile."

"But don't you get lonesome?" I knew something of the loneliness that brings on cabin fever. I had seen what it could do to a man.

"I ain't got time to get very lonesome. Besides there's the dogs for company and sometimes Johnny Busia stops by. Every now and then somebody comes up the creek—like you. And it's only a few miles to the Red Top Mine."

The Red Top Mine, I later learned, was a big one that worked crews and even ran a swing shift. It was a stock mine and Fannie was one of the biggest shareholders. "They got a radio," she said. "I can call out for anything I want and Frank Pollock will fly it in."

"Suppose you get sick, or have an accident?"

"I take care of myself when I'm sick. If I have a bad accident maybe I can take care of that, too. Like I did for Joe."

Her husband, Joe, had gone out to Nenana, a hundred miles away, on business. He had decided to fly back. The roar of the plane's motor had wakened Fannie early one morning. She jumped out of bed and looked out the window just in time to see the plane hit the gravel bar on Moose Creek, bounce high in the air and land on its nose in the middle of the creek.

She had run down there and found Joe and two other men crawling out of the plane. Joe was the only one hurt. His face was a mass of blood. His nose had been split lengthwise clear through and hung in two halves. She led him up to the cabin, washed him up, got out her needle and thread and sewed the nose together.

"I never sewed up anybody before," she said. "And a nose was kind of a prominent place to begin. I pulled the two halves nice and snug and sewed them the way I do my moccasins. I used an over and under stitch, which is the way you sew a baseball."

"Did it heal?" I asked.

"Just fine," she said proudly. "I told a doctor about it later in Fairbanks and he said I sewed it all wrong. But the nose never gave Joe any trouble so I guess my stitching was all right.

"But that wasn't bad," she ran on lightly. "Joe could still walk. It's when you can't walk that it's tough up here. I'll never forget the time Joe was working in a tunnel on the other side of the mountain about eight miles from here. It was too far to come home every night so he was baching there in a tent. I would go over every few days with the dogs packed with grub."

This day there had been no sign of life. Fannie pushed into the tent and there was Joe stretched out on the floor unconscious. His hip and one shoulder were broken from an accident in the mine. She splint the hip as best she knew how, then managed to wrestle him onto the cot.

She hiked miles across country to get help from a pair of miners working on another creek. One of the miners headed for the railroad to call out a plane and doctor for Joe. Fannie and the other carried Joe four miles to the gravel bar on Moose Creek where the plane could land.

"That was pretty bad, Joe busted up like he was, and us shaking him at every step," she said. "Joe was 'gone' more than half a year that time. That's the kind of accidents you got to watch out for. I got practically a medicine chest that will take care of cuts and bruises and just plain getting sick."

After we had washed the dishes she helped me dismantle the starvation claim for the planks. I tried to thank her for them and the dinner, but she waved my thanks aside. "I was glad to have you. Come down when you can. I can always rustle up something to eat."

I saw Fannie often. A two-hour hike is "just next door" in the North. She would come trudging up the creek, rifle across her arm. "You getting rich yet, Jack?" was her standard greeting. She never called me by any other name and she refused to treat my mining venture as anything but a joke. The fact that I was taking out slightly more than an ounce a day meant nothing to her. She had decided the creek was hungry ground. Nothing short of a stampede would change her mind.

Fannie's occasional visits were my salvation those days. While I was used to being alone when mining in Idaho, I could always hike to a nearby town when I wanted people. Here I was a hundred miles from nowhere and pressed for time. Day after day the only breaks in that vast silence were the sounds of an occasional bird, the murmur of the creek, and the scratching of my pick and shovel. The very sight of Mt. McKinley looking eternally down on me became annoying. It was like a long, cool drink just to see Fannie's hunched-up little figure, her rifle across her knees, sitting on the bank watching me, to hear her voice grumble, "Jack, when did you eat your last square meal?" And before I could answer— "No man can do that work on beans and bacon. You come down tonight and get a square meal under your belt."

Many a night I have tramped back up the dark trail from her cabin, stuffed with good food and carrying an extra parcel of bread or doughnuts under my arm.

On one of her trips she tossed me a moose-hide poke she had made. "If you're going to scrabble around in this hungry ground you might as well have something to keep those few grains of dust in," she said. By now I had discovered her rough speech was a cover-up to hide the softhearted Fannie beneath.

Fannie lived ninety per cent off the land. To do so she accomplished an amazing number of things that would have put to shame many a husky man. During the short summer weeks and fall she was busy as a squirrel packing away for winter.

She had several tunnels driven into the hill near the cabin. One was in perma-frost, with doors to keep the heat out. In it she kept her meat, frozen the year round. Here also, she

had stacks of baked bread, pies and doughnuts. The second
tunnel was in thawed gravel with double doors to keep the
cold out. Here she kept her potatoes, vegetables and fruit.
Fannie often amazed her guests in the dead of winter, by
serving them fresh vegetables from her tunnel.

During the summer she picked gallons of wild blueberries
and cranberries and made them into jams and jellies. She
gathered great armloads of wild grass, dried it, and stored
it away for the dogs' bedding, for her own as well as for
visitors' dogs. Sometimes, with trappers and rangers from
McKinley Park stopping by, there might be as many as
eighteen or twenty dogs tied about the cabin.

Fall came with startling swiftness. At least it seemed swift
to one used to the long, slowly shortening days, the gradual
dying of leaves and grass on Idaho's hills and valleys. Here,
I could see the days snipping away the hours of light. The
lengthening hours of night cut time from my working day.
But I was still taking out my ounce a shift and I had ripped
a huge hole in the gravel bar.

One day Fannie trudged up and announced, "Caribou will
be coming through tomorrow or next day." How she knew
I could not guess.

"When you want to go after some, let me know. I'll take
a day off and help you," I offered.

She shook her head. "You got plenty to do, and not much
time left to do it in. I'll get my caribou. I don't need any
help." My face apparently showed doubt and she added, "I
out-hunted Joe more than once, and he was good." Sitting
cross-legged on the bank, her old hands locked about the
rifle barrel, she told me of one of those times.

Game had been mighty scarce that fall. She and Joe hunted

several days with no luck. Then one afternoon they split up. Joe went one way, Fannie another. During the afternoon she killed two caribou, a bear and a moose. She dressed them out before Joe arrived. Next morning she tossed him her skirt and said, "Here, you do the housework. I'm the hunter in this family. Gimme your pants."

"It took him a month to get over that," she chuckled.

Fannie's humor was rough and ready. I had heard the story a missionary told on himself. He and a bush pilot had been caught in a storm and landed on the gravel bar near Fannie's; they spent several days as her guests. For supper one evening she cooked up her favorite caribou stew. The pilot loaded his plate and dug in. The missionary carefully picked out the meat explaining to Fannie, "This is Friday. I never eat meat on Friday, you know."

Fannie disappeared only to return with a head of lettuce, "Here, eat grass," she snapped. "All the rabbits do."

When the missionary left he tried to pay her but she refused. "I'll send you a case of chocolate," he promised. "What is your favorite brand?"

"Schlitz," Fannie answered promptly.

The day after her visit I was busy shoveling gravel into the sluice box when I heard splashing in the creek. A hundred feet off two caribou were unhurriedly wading the stream. I dived up the bank for the rifle. When I swung about, a half-dozen more had emerged and were browsing along on tufts of grass and moss. It looked more like a pasture scene of contented cows with tremendous horns than wild game. I waited for the old excitement of the hunt to pick me up. It did not come. I watched them cross the creek and disappear.

Then I knew why. After charging brown bears, whales and killer whales these awkward, leisurely animals left me cold.

Day and night for two weeks, caribou were all about me, forty thousand strong by government count. They came singly, in pairs, in bunches, then as a solid mass moving across the land. The complete Northern stillness came alive with the clashing of horns, the rolling of rocks along the creek beds and slopes. Their long, homely faces showed one common expression, sadness. They tramped along, head down, ponderous, as though the worries of the world rested on their broad antlers.

Several times I heard the crack of Fannie's rifle as she harvested her winter's meat. Fat bear for lard and cooking, but for meat—caribou, moose and whatever small animals suited her fancy. She skinned her kills swiftly, deftly as any butcher, cut them up and carried the meat on her back to her deep-freeze tunnel. Several times I caught glimpses of her small figure, bent almost double under some load of meat.

One afternoon I knocked off early and hiked down to visit Fannie. I met her a half mile from the cabin with a load. I took it from her and asked, half joking, "You kill a moose?"

She straightened and wiped sweat from her eyes with a sleeve, "A moose and two bear since sun-up," she announced proudly.

"I'll help you dress them."

"That's all done, and half the meat is in the tunnel. That is the last of the bear you've got."

Here was a woman old enough to be a grandmother, an old grandmother at that, and to outward appearances a fragile one. What she needed was a rocking chair in the shade, with her knitting or a grandchild on her knee. I told her so.

She gave me a whimsical smile. "You think I would look good at that, Jack?"

I tried to fit her into the picture. It was no use. This was where she belonged, leaning on her rifle in a trail, surrounded by miles of virgin wilderness, her wrinkled old face aglow with the success of the hunt.

She said almost gently, "Let's carry the meat in, Jack."

I heaved it to my shoulder. "You must have enough for winter," I said. "Quit trying to kill yourself."

"Enough for me, sure," she said with a mischievous grin, "but not enough for all you bums that stop by."

She was right, but we both knew she would have it no other way. Fannie's hospitality was famous. "Be sure you stop by Fannie's," an old sourdough had told me in Anchorage. "You'll never eat a meal like hers again in this man's world."

It was surprising the number of people who have visited her in this remote district over the years. There were big-game hunters, explorers, missionaries, prospectors and mountain climbers. She had been hostess to practically every successful or unsuccessful party assaulting Mt. McKinley since 1910. Being entertained en route by Fannie was an event the climbers looked forward to.

While Fannie hunted, and gradually filled her larder, I worked from daylight to dark on the "Never Sweat" claim. The moose-hide poke she gave me slowly filled with bright yellow dust. Mine was no strike. It was not even a prosperous claim. But I was making it pay, and like many fishermen and boatmen, I was working off the glamour of mining in the far North. Gold is gold, and mining is work and sweat, no matter where or how you do it.

The sun still shone but now it held a hard, brassy shine that lacked its former warmth. The air turned crisp as celery stalks. Each night was a trifle colder than the one before. Mt. McKinley's white height wore a chill, forbidding look. On her last trip up, Fannie announced that her storage tunnels were filled. There was still the lard to render from one bear. She had split a half-dozen cords of wood. Now she was working on her traps. She meant to run a couple of trap lines during the winter. Before she left she warned me, "When we get the first hard freeze you get out, unless you want to stay through the winter."

That day arrived less than a week later. One morning ice was frozen solid in the sluice box. Unlike my home in the States, here the weather would become swiftly colder with no let-up. Soon the ground would be frozen and ice would make the sluice box useless. My mining venture was over.

I hauled the sluice box up on the bank, rolled my pack and left. The moose-hide poke was full. I was satisfied.

On the way out I stopped to tell Fannie good-by. The dogs sat spaced about the cabin as always, panting in the late afternoon sun. Fannie was rendering the last of the bear lard and the kitchen was greasy-hot. She came to the doorway, stuffing wisps of gray hair under a stocking-leg cap. She still wore the choke-bore pants and shoe pacs. "Figured you would be along today or tomorrow. You're quitting just in time. Well," she smiled, "you get rich, Jack?"

I handed her the round, full moose-hide poke and she weighed it expertly in her hand. "About twenty-five ounces. You did good—considering." She handed it back. "Guess that means I'll be seeing you next year."

"I don't know," I said.

"You've got gold dust in your blood now," she said matter-of-factly. "You've got the Kantishna in it, too, but you don't know that yet. About January you'll start thinking of these hills, the creeks, the long days and short nights, how the sun goes down and the look of McKinley on a clear day, and how the caribou come through. Oh, you'll be back."

I glanced about the snug kitchen where I had eaten so many fine meals, at the Yukon stove, the anvil surrounded by rusty pick heads, the rough shelves loaded with ore samples. Suddenly I knew I would never see it again. I tried to thank her but she waved my words aside. "You were a good neighbor, Jack. I'll be seeing you."

I went past the grinning dogs, past the now barren rock-terraced garden and down the trail. At the bottom of the bench I glanced back. Against towering McKinley the cabin looked like a toy, the figure in the doorway a very small, rather badly worn doll. I remembered her words, "There's not a hill or valley here I haven't left my boot prints on. I'll die here, Jack."

I felt depressed until I thought of all the people she had befriended over the years, the others who told stories of her exploits in Anchorage, Fairbanks, Nome. Those stories would become greater with the passage of time. So long as one man lived to repeat them the blithe spirit of Fannie the Hike would roam her beloved Kantishna hills.

17

Boots and Saddles and Deep-Sea Men

I had never given a thought to the sort of music the Alaskan fishermen might enjoy, until that spring my brother-in-law, Norvin Greek, went North with me. Norvin is a musician with a fine voice. He insisted on taking along two guitars, an amplifier and P.A. system. "I can play in some of those bars. We can put out a hat or something for a donation kitty. We might pick up fifty or sixty dollars a night. You know what I did down here."

"But this is Idaho," I said. "We're going to Alaska."

"So much the better," he argued. "They must be starved for music."

There was no arguing him out of it, so the instruments went along.

It was a good year for everyone connected with the fishing industry. The run was one of the biggest in years. Seiners came in loaded down with fish—and so did the pirates. The canneries put up one of the biggest packs on record.

It was a good year for diving, too. There was an unusually large number of call-back dives. Between calls we raised a

246

sunken boat that had crashed a trap and sunk, recovered a pair of lost motors and raised a ton of steel shafting for the Army.

It was a bad season for Norvin and his music. He had no chance to make town on a week end when the fishing fleet was in because we were always working. The few times we came in it was the middle of the week and the town was deserted.

The short, thirty-day season passed swiftly. All too soon the day came when the cannery boats made the rounds of the traps notifying the watchmen that the Bureau of Fisheries had set the date for closing and that on a certain hour all traps must stop fishing.

The end of season is a dramatic time. Men came out from the canneries and swarmed over the pile traps cutting down the wire. The pile extractor moved in and began yanking out the piling. On the floaters, the anchors were hauled up and the traps towed ashore where the wire was stripped away and the bare frame of the trap left standing, waiting another season. In a matter of days there was no sign that a floating trap or a piling trap had ever been opposite Woodcock Point or Bligh Island.

Part of the fishing fleet prepared to tie up for the winter in Cordova or Valdez. Some would head south for Ketchikan, or on farther to Seattle. Some would go to California, as far south as the Gulf, to fish tuna for several months.

I hung around waiting for one last dive. I finally got it at Valdez when I raised a load of pipe for the Army.

That night, as we sat in the galley cooking supper, Norvin asked, "We're about through diving, aren't we?"

"We are through," I said. "Tomorrow we start getting ready to go home."

After a minute he asked, "How many bars in this town?"

"Four or five. Why?" I asked. But I knew why. He had not had his night to make music and he still wanted it.

"They ought to be crowded now that the season's over. I'll probably never come North again and I would like to leave in a blaze of glory. Let's take the instruments uptown and give the citizens a farewell serenade."

After supper, loaded down with musical equipment we trudged uptown and into one of Valdez's biggest restaurants. I chose Carl and Edna's Bar because I knew they had a banquet room—in case the crowd got big. Carl was a brawny fellow who once had been a fisherman. He worked the front and Edna did the cooking. Carl said, "Music? We can always go for good music."

We set the amplifier in the street doorway and shoved a pair of tables together in the middle of the room to make a musician's stand. Norvin sat on top of the tables, drifted his fingers across the strings, then swung into "Wabash Cannon Ball." The notes of the guitar and Norvin's voice poured into the quiet street:

> "She come down to Birmingham
> One cold December day.
> As she pulled into the station
> You could hear all the people say,
> 'Here's a gal from Tennessee,
> She's long and she's tall.
> She come down to Birmingham
> On the Wabash Cannon Ball.' "

Before the song was ended the mob began pouring in. Norvin was right, these people were hungry for music. I hunted up the biggest cigar box I could find and put it in plain sight on top of the piano for the kitty.

Swanie came shoving through the crowd, rubbing his red nose and grinning happily. "What are you doing here?" I asked.

"You ain't heard? I got my own boat," he said proudly.

I had seen his boat, an old relic he had resurrected from some beach and over the winter had put in working order. She was about twenty-six feet and would carry a couple of thousand fish.

"I heard the music down at the dock and just started to run." He moved me aside, "Get away, man, I got a job here." He climbed to the table top beside Norvin, plunked down a chair and dragged a battered harmonica from his pocket.

They swung into "When the Bloom Is On the Sage." Swanie was good. Here I had known him for years and was not even aware that he carried a harmonica.

The crowd kept coming. Every bar in town must have emptied. We moved the chairs and tables out of the banquet hall to make more room. George Gregaroff, a half-Indian, half-Russian boy, played the Spanish guitar. George was about eighteen and worked as a deck hand aboard the fish boats. He was a frail dark-haired boy with features delicate as a girl's. He hunched over the guitar, slender fingers brushing the strings. The three went through "Silver-Haired Daddy of Mine," "I Got Spurs That Jingle Jangle Jingle," "The Old Chisholm Trail"—cowboy stuff for deep-sea jockeys.

The music grew louder as the crowd increased. A big fisherman made a stab at playing the piano, held on a couple of minutes, then gave up. A couple of women sang. A man tried, but after a bellowing start, forgot the words. When someone else was not trying to sing Norvin was.

I kept one eye on the drunks, herding them off the musician's stand, and the other on the kitty that was swelling to mouth-watering proportions. Some fishermen were tossing bills in there and they were not the dollar kind. There was laughter and shouting, the clink of glasses, the shuffle of feet. The principal talk, as always, had to do with fish and fishing. In a corner, several men argued loudly over the size of the year's run. A couple of others bragged about a pirate haul that had come in the last day of season. Another man was trying to work up a deal to buy a boat. At the bar two watchmen listened intently as a big fisherman explained, "You guys work with me next season and I'll send you outside with an extra two thousand dollars each in your suitcases."

The jam got tighter. Someone offered Edna and Carl a drink. They took it because this was the end of season and everyone was happy.

Voices became loud in one corner. Fists began flying as two men milled about trying to punch each other in the tight press of bodies. The disturbance surged toward the door. I got behind and kept them going through the door into the street. Part of the crowd poured out to cheer the fighters on. For a minute I watched them scuffling and flailing at each other, then I went back inside.

I was watching the kitty when the fighters returned arm in arm, followed by the crowd. The fighters were given a drink and leaned against the bar side by side. The bigger was going to have a black eye in the morning. The smaller man's mouth was swollen and the back of his head was bloody.

The bloody-headed one said, "Hitting me when I slipped was okay. But you shouldn't have pounded my head on the sidewalk."

"If you hadn't slipped you wouldn't have got your head pounded," the big man told him.

"Well, that's so. But it's no way to fight."

"The hell it ain't. You might as well admit now that a good little man can't lick a good big one."

"I'm not so sure. I was doing all right until I slipped."

"You're crazy as a loon."

"No, the slip saved your bacon."

"Why, you conceited damn fool," the big man said, "do I have to take you outside and show you all over again?"

"I guess maybe you do."

They disappeared back outside, followed by the few nearest them who had heard their words. This time they did not return.

Edna passed out, and people began clamoring for something to eat. I found her sitting in a corner of the kitchen, propped upright by a circle of chairs, staring straight ahead. Carl had disappeared, no one seemed to know where. I peeled out of my coat and took over the kitchen.

Edna would have had fits at sight of the feeds I turned out and Carl would have gone mad at the prices I charged. I sold the works—spuds, gravy, meat, vegetables, pie, coffee—to a young fellow for a dime. He was a deck hand on a boat that had been laid up most of the season after crashing a rock. I charged another, who I knew had been pirating and had taken several ten-thousand-fish loads, ten dollars for a sandwich.

He was about two-thirds drunk and when I told him the price he calmly opened the sandwich and began poking through it with a fork. "Don't want to bust my teeth on all them gold nuggets," he explained amiably. But he paid me.

I sold dinners for a quarter, half a dollar. I looked over each customer, figured his ability to pay and charged accordingly. Had there not been the music and plenty to drink, which gave this party an air of celebration, I am sure some of those prices would have backfired in flying knuckles.

I sold out the kitchen to the bare shelves. The cash register bulged until I could no longer close the till and a wad of bills puffed out the half-open drawer.

Carl never re-appeared, and sometime during the evening Edna was carried off to bed. For all practical purposes the place was mine.

Swanie eventually joined the revelers. With the kitchen out of food I joined in too. Even Norvin was leaving the musician's stand between numbers.

It was getting light when the crowd finally began to trickle out. At last there were just the four of us left. Norvin, Swanie and George split a hundred-and-thirty-dollar kitty and called it a night. We hauled the instruments into a corner to be picked up later. I took a last look around, at the empty banquet room, the kitchen stacked high with dirty dishes, the cash register with the till half open and the bills bursting out. There were empty bottles and glasses everywhere. The musician's stand stood vacant with a pair of chairs in the middle. The place looked lonesome and deserted.

I hooked an arm through one of Swanie's, Norvin took

the other. I snapped the night lock on the front door, closed it, and we set off through the chill dawn, half dragging Swanie between us.

At the dock we discovered the tide was out and it was forty feet down to the deck of Swanie's boat. In his condition we knew he would never negotiate the slimy ladder nailed to the face of the dock. We found a length of rope, tied one end about Swanie's middle and lowered him over the edge. We ran out of rope with a good ten feet yet to go. We snubbed the rope about a cleat and went in search of more. Swanie came awake and began singing at the top of his lungs, "Oh-h-h, I'm a-heading for the last wind-up. Oh boy, oh boy, oh-h-h-h boy. . . ."

There was no more rope. We tried to haul Swanie up, but he was too heavy. Our efforts only woke him more and he bellowed louder.

Norvin called, "Swanie, we haven't enough rope to let you down and we can't haul you up. What shall we do?"

"That's okay," Swanie yelled. "Just let go the rope. Just let me go. Oh-h-h-h, I'm a-heading for the las-s-s-s-s—" We let go the rope and walked away. Swanie's song chopped off in a thud.

When we woke, after about four hours sleep Norvin said, "This is the day we head for home."

"This is the day we begin getting ready to go home," I corrected. "I have to take the boat back to the cannery and collect my diving money. That will take a day. Crating the diving suit and compressor will take another." I had been thinking of something else, too. The thud when Swanie landed on deck. "There was a lot of gear on that old boat," I said. "What if Swanie landed on it?"